Black Exodus
The Great Migration from the American South

Black
Exodus

The Great Migration
from the American South

Edited by Alferdteen Harrison

University Press of Mississippi
Jackson and London

94 93 92 91 4 3 2 1

The paper in this book meets the guidelines for permanence
and durability of the Committee on Production Guidelines
for Book Longevity of the Council on Library Resources.

Library of Congress Cataloging-in-Publication Data

Black exodus : the great migration from the American South / essays by
    Dernoral Davis . . . [et al.] ; edited by Alferdteen Harrison.
        p.   cm.
    Includes index.
    ISBN 0–87805–491–X (alk. paper)
    1. Afro-Americans—Migrations—History—20th century.
    2. Migration, Internal—United States—History—20th century.
    3. Southern States—Race relations. 4. Southern States—Population—
    History—20th century. I. Davis, Dernoral. II. Harrison, Alferdteen.
E185.6.B6251991
305.896′073075—dc20   90–192
                                                                          CI

British Library Cataloging-in-Publication data available

Contents

Preface

The "Great Migration" is as important in the study of African-American history as are the Civil War and the civil rights movement. Older African-Americans generally remember when an aunt, uncle, cousin or close friend left the South to go to school or to find a job in northern industries. Some remember or have heard of a person who had to leave because of violence in the segregated society. Even though almost all southern African-American families and communities have been touched in some way by the "Great Migration," few understand the multiple southern forces that created it.

During the "Great Migration," 1915 to 1960, about five million rural southern African-Americans migrated to the northern industrialized cities of America. The immediate conditions for the "Great Migration" were created after the Civil War when African-Americans were not given "forty acres and a mule," the means of economic survival at that time. Intensifying the deprived status of the African-American was the system of legal segregation that gradually emerged throughout the South after the 1896 Plessy vs. Ferguson Supreme Court Decision legalizing separate railroad accommodations. Legal segregation aborted the trend to recognize the citizenship rights of African-Americans that had begun thirty-one years earlier with the Emancipation Proclamation and continued with the passage of the thirteenth, fourteenth, and fifteenth Amendments. Segregation presented many contradictions to American democracy, particularly in the South where more than five million African-Americans decided to leave in search of a better life.

Though much of the scholarship on the Great Migration has cited the forces of southern racial oppression as a cause for it, these forces have not been previously analyzed. Focusing on the South, the essays in this book discuss some of the forces that emerged in the segregated lifestyle of the South and encouraged the "Great Migration." Primary among these were: the use of the myth of white racial superiority to justify and enforce segregation through overt hostility and lynchings; the idling African-American labor in the South because of increasing white job competition as industrialization and agricultural mechanization came to the South; the work opportunities in the war industries in the north; and the relocation of large numbers of African-Americans from areas where they had lost hope of bettering their conditions. Though a prevalent response to the conditions created by the "segregation creed" was the migration, many responded by using the migration to leverage improved conditions for African-Americans.

The conditions and causes discussed in these essays analyze the African-American's search for an acceptable status in America, the role of racial violence, as well as social and economic forces in the South that encouraged the migration. Also discussed are southern white reactions to the loss of their labor and the use of the migration by both northern and southern African-American leaders to achieve social change. The last three essays present fresh perspectives on the origins of the recent struggle for social change and the current status of the African-American in the south.

In the introduction Blyden Jackson, provides a conceptual perspective from which to view the migration and illustrates that the cause for the "Great Migration" was the African-American's continuing pilgrimage in search of an acceptable status in America. The pilgrimage had its origin in the fifteenth century with the beginning of the African diaspora and modern slavery before the birth of America. Jackson asserts that because the status of the African-American as a slave and then as a "Jim Crow" citizen were unacceptable, the migration was a continuation of the search.

Dernoral Davis's essay, "Toward a Socio-Historical and Demographic Portrait of Twentieth-Century African-Americans," gives an historical overview of the twentieth century evolution of the African-American through the 1980 census. It provides significant information about the makeup of the African-American population, and the impact of the migration, growth patterns, fertility, and mortality rate on that population. Davis concludes that the most important demographic changes for African-Americans have been in the areas of sex ratios, marital status, and, consequently, family and household patterns.

In their essay "Rethinking the Role of Racial Violence in the Great Migration," Stewart E. Tolnay and E. M. Beck explain the economic and social causes for the out-migration, using the cotton states of Georgia and South Carolina as case studies. Though lynching is presented as a method of social control, the reciprocal relationship between black migration and racial violence is illustrated. The essay illustrates the role that white competition for jobs had in encouraging the migration.

Carole Marks addresses the subtle economic changes that African-Americans faced as a result of the South's industrial transformation. At the turn of century, northern investors in the South sought to aid the industrial developers who hired poor whites instead of African-American artisans who were either not allowed to train for semiskilled and skilled jobs or were brutally forced to join the farm tenant system. The essay provides an interesting discussion of the African-American laborers who were performing the dirtiest and lowest paying jobs or were unemployed and ready to migrate when the opportunity came.

James R. Grossman's " 'Black Labor Is the Best Labor': Southern White Reactions to the Great Migration," develops the central theme that whites generally did not recognize or reconcile themselves to the challenge that the migration posed to their values. The essay documents two kinds of group responses, those wanting African-Americans to leave and those who developed agendas for change in order to encourage African-Americans to stay. Even this latter group addressed symptoms of dissatisfaction instead of the economic and social relations between whites and blacks.

"The Great Migration as a Lever for Social Change," by William Cohen presents the national response to the Great Migration by discussing how the African-American community used the migration to create positions for select persons in the federal government. This essay focuses on the period between 1917 and 1919 when both the national government and the members of the African-American community were interested in studying the impact of the migration.

In somewhat the same vein as Cohen, Neil McMillen suggests that African-Americans in Mississippi used the migration to gain social advances. "The Migration and Black Protest in Jim Crow Mississippi," presents a contrast to the image of the passive African-American who was too "suppressed" to migrate. McMillen asserts that African-Americans began to play an active protest role after World War I that continued throughout the 1960s.

The Great Migration was the subject of a symposium held at Jackson State University in September 1989. More than twenty-two noted scholars presented papers or comments in conjunction with the Smithsonian Institution's "From Field to Factory" traveling exhibition that was housed at the Smith Robertson Museum. The exhibit focused on the causes for the migration, the process of leaving, and the arrival in and adjustment of African-Americans to northern urban communities. A companion exhibit at Smith Robertson Museum concentrated on those Mississippians who did not migrate.

For their support in making possible the symposium and exhibit, I would like to thank the National Endowment for the Humanities, the Mississippi Humanities Council, the Smithsonian Institution's Traveling Exhibition Services, Jackson State University, and last but not least the staff of JSU's Margaret Walker Alexander National Research Center for the Study of the Twentieth-Century African-American.

Blyden Jackson

Introduction: A Street of Dreams

It has been a long, long time, more than 500 years, since a young Portuguese mariner named Antam Gonçalvez captured some stray Africans around 1442 and took them back with him to his home port in Portugal as slaves. Inasmuch as Gonçalvez was negotiating waters off the west coast of Africa he may well be considered the unwitting beginner of the Atlantic slave trade. So, too, to him, conceivably, may be traced everything pertaining to black America, not excluding that hopeful trek, lasting approximately thirty years (about the extent of a human generation), of black Southerners from the South to the North that historians of black America sometimes call the Great Migration.

The Atlantic slave trade did bring some Negroes directly from Africa to our America, although far fewer than most people seem to think. The first black permanent residents of our America lived in Tidewater, Virginia—in other words, in the South. They actually did precede the Pilgrims, being left at Jamestown in 1619. There were, apparently, only twenty of them. Their consanguineous descendants here now number in excess of twenty-six million, about three million more than the number of residents our last census-takers were able to discover in California, America's most populous state. It may be tempting, therefore, to picture to one's self a great influx of blacks from Africa into the United States after the deposit of the Jamestown Negroes and consequently to postulate that in black America, there is the powerful presence of an

African atavism. One could believe that this atavism is perpetuated, if by nothing else, by the aggregation of African-rooted recollections and practices in acquired behavior of millions of black Americans who were born and spent their formative years in Africa and who preserved and passed on African culture to black American children (who then passed them on to their children). But such has not been the case. Careful analysis of the slave trade demonstrates that, at the highest possible extreme, no more than 600,000 black Africans were ever delivered to the United States from 1619 until the middle 1860s (when the last slaves beached in North America) with no intervening "seasoning"—almost all of them, incidentally, before the end of the eighteenth century. "Seasoning," in the present context, refers to the training in Western enslavement received by a native African in the West Indies (or, in rare instances, elsewhere) before a transfer to the American mainland. It added only negligibly to the total of native Africans who ended their separation from their homelands within our America.

Even so, there have long been efforts by interested parties both within and without the select community of scholars to argue that there is a significant persistence of African traditions and artifacts (including language) in black America, particularly in that class and breed of black Americans often alluded to as "the black folk." To deny, with no proof, any possibility of African survivals in the present racial inheritance of black Americans, folk or otherwise, would certainly be to commit a grievous error. Moreover, in at least one isolated instance, that of the Gullah people, who have long been largely sequestered from other Americans in islands along the Atlantic coast from, roughly, Charleston, South Carolina, to Savannah, Georgia, the evidence of the existence of African survivals is too palpable to be ignored. Yet the phenomenon of provenience (where people came from) forces upon us a conclusion about the tremendous expansion in size of black America which can, in no wise, be refuted. That conclusion tells us, simply and clearly, that the main cause, by far, for black America's enormous growth is natural increase—that is, black births in America. Negroes situated on American soil have long been parenting children where they have lived much or all of their lives. These children have been doing as did their parents. This procreation of American blacks by American blacks has been going on for well over three hundred years. In that entire lengthy period of time no subtractions which would notably reduce the population of black America have occurred, whether, as examples, in the nineteenth century as a result of subsidies or forms of coercion or persuasion initiated by the pro-slavery colonizationists or in this century as a response to Marcus Garvey's clarion call to black Americans to return to Africa.

The psyches and ethos of black Americans, accordingly, with no exception that matters, have been formed and dominated by an American environment. This incontrovertible fact must be given its due weight in any attempt to properly appreciate the black American's Great Migration. One needs, in short, to apprehend how fully and unalterably American the American Negro truly is to detect with a sufficiently perspicacious eye the deeper currents of passion that metamorphosed into marching orders the fondest dream of the Southern black and energized his feet when he willed himself to forsake the South and travel north. He wanted, in that most candid expression of himself, one thing only, to enjoy America. He did not want to trade the values he had come to cherish in a country native to him for those of any other nationality or culture. He merely wanted to make come true for himself what he believed he could see had already come true for virtually all other Americans, particularly in the respect paid to their dignity as persons and in the access allowed them to seek political and economic well-being among their fellow Americans. To speak in terms unequivocal, yet most accurate for him, he wanted to be more completely and more unrestrictedly American.

This desperate, gnawing yearning of his to fare in America at least as well as other Americans was, as it were, terribly intensified by the circumstance that he was not only so American. He was also very southern. As late as 1900, slightly more than nine of every ten inhabitants of black America still lived in the South. Theirs was, as is well-known, the South which had fought a bloody, savage war to keep blacks enslaved. In general this South was, as it had always been, about as great an antithesis to the ideal America for black people as could possibly be imagined. But even its racism was far from all about the South that Southern blacks could not abide. The South, even apart from the paranoia of its program of white supremacy, in comparison with the North, where a vigorous exploitation of the industrial revolution had produced a community vibrant with optimism and material progress, was a woefully antiquated social order too feudally agrarian for its own good. With or without slavery, this South was not the section of America where the future (or the present) seemed to show its brightest promise. The South had been appallingly static before it fired on Fort Sumter. Nothing about it after its surrender at Appomattox seemed essentially to have changed. It was narcotized by its worship of its golden myth of its antebellum self as a benign aristocracy. And its so-called Redemption following the era of Reconstruction could only be construed as what it unquestionably was, a resolute attempt to resurrect the past and return its race relations to the days of Calhoun and of masters and overseers. But, no less to its detriment, it lagged, in its whole way of life, behind the North. It was the North, as America entered a new century, into which capital, invention, entrepreneurial ingenuity, immigrants from overseas, and the might of corporate endeavor poured. It was the North which boomed, the North which, race aside, was bettering its preferential position to the South. It was the North where, apparently, everything was moving on.

News about this North, as was to be expected, constantly filtered down to southern Negroes. They could not but feel a strong inclination to test the veracity of the reports they received about it. As soon, then, as the late 1870s and early 1880s they launched their first attempt to make their way into this fabled Canaan. They chose as their initial point of entry the state of Kansas. A patriarchal black Tennessean, one "Pap" Singleton, took the lead in exhorting them into an exodus which gained for those who joined in it the sobriquet of "Exodusters." But all did not turn out for these "Exodusters" quite as had been hoped. That which they had pictured to themselves as mainly a potential crystal stair eventuated too extensively into a trail of tears. Nevertheless, their fate in Kansas, mixed as it was, diminished little, if at all, the general enthusiasm of southern Negroes for moving to the North.

So, as time continued on its way, Southern Negroes continued to steal away from the South. In 1914 came the assassination of an Austrian archduke, which precipitated World War I, thereby occasioning, as one side effect, a sudden and drastic decline in European emigration to America at precisely a moment when northern captains of industry and finance, recipients of huge contracts to supply their favored combatants with munitions and other emergency requirements for nations involved in modern war, experienced a need to quickly expand a labor force. Correlatively, the steady trickle of southern blacks into the North grew to a flood, thus creating, among other things, the classical black ghettos of urban America above the Mason–Dixon Line. As America (after recruiting two armies, one white and one black, to fight in World War I) entered the 1920s it found itself coexisting with women's suffrage, prohibition, bootlegging, the automobile age, radio, movie moguls and Hollywood stars, a burgeoning Babbittry, flappers, flush times for a while on Wall Street, a Lost Generation in literature and the arts, a new freedom for its youth, and the beginning of the end of any bucolic simplicites it had ever had. Concurrently, in black America, Harlem in Manhattan, the South Side in Chicago, and Paradise Valley in Detroit reached the peak of their prosperity, as did smaller replicas throughout the North of these cities within cities largely populated by the Great Migration and its offspring. But the northward surge of the southern Negro had crested by the end of the 1920s. It would never again be so high. Ahead of it, as of all America, in the womb of unknown time, were the worst depression yet in American history, a second and bigger World War and our America of today, a miracle of modern science with powers for both good and evil beyond the wildest fantasies of any human creatures but those living now.

Inevitably, Negro literature bears within itself content, as well as themes and moods, reflecting the Great Migration. Indeed, it probably may be safely said that no other event, large or small, which competent students recognize as a valid part of black America's past has had an impact equal in mass or gravity upon the consciousness of black writers. Richard Wright's *Native Son*, for example, is steeped in the world of the Great Migration, as is the poetry of Gwendolyn Brooks and the drama of Lorraine

Hansberry. Actually, as of now, two successive generations of Negro writers and the beginning of a third have found the most abundant source of the material they have used in the Great Migration, if not literally in the migrants themselves and their deeds, then, in the special conditions left by the migrants to their descendants, the world which we may call, not too arbitrarily, the aftermath of the Great Migration. It may well be in truth that black writers have said even more about this aftermath than about the Great Migration itself. In so doing, it can be added, they have tended more toward commiseration than joy. They have perceived, in effect, a sequel to the Great Migration in its totality too exact a copy of the frustrations of the Exodusters in Kansas. They have been much aware of the slum housing, the school dropouts, the widespread chronic unemployment, the high incidence of vice, crime and violence and worse, perhaps, of all, the increase, statistically, of a dispossessed underclass in precisely those highways and byways of the North where once, while our century was young, uprooted southern Negroes settled to improve their lot. Black literature certainly is not satisfied with the northern aftermath of the Great Migration to which it has devoted so much of its time and its published work.

Still, all that southern blacks were hoping to attain through their Great Migration should not be deemed, apparently, to have been lost. The North is surely not as bad for Negroes as the South the Great Migration fled. Nor has change, either in race relations or otherwise, been so absent lately in the South as once it was. Jim Crow is gone. An amelioration of discrimination, as well as of segregation, has occurred. But also, not necessarily because of any changes connected with race, the sectionalism so long a barrier between the South and North apparently is vanishing as utterly as a whisper in the wind, too utterly, some people, especially some people of artistic bent, lament. There is a term, appreciably current now, which does convey a sense both of a radical elimination of variety in America (which may well be real) and of the aversion of Americans to whom diversity can be possessed of value to the implied meanings of this term. The term, itself, is "homogenization." It suggests an America wherein a vast sameness rules, a duplication by every integer of every other integer taxonomically its mate. And, it must be conceded, homogenization does appear to be rife in our America. All the cities with their shopping centers, supermarkets and subdivisions (which all look alike), all the airports, all the anchorpersons on the television new shows, all the cheerleaders, all the people on the street, all the entertainers, all the anything, look, and do, alike. In any case, former disparities no longer suggest a better life for blacks (or whites) in the North rather than the South. With the changes in race relations in the South and the effect upon America of homogenization, it is no wonder then that currently an episode in black history is repeating itself in reverse. The Great Migration has turned around and is returning to the South.

From March 1985, until March 1988, of blacks in America, 586,385 went from the North back to the South. In these same three years, only 326,842 blacks followed the original pattern of the Great Migration and went from the South to the North. Moreover, quite interestingly, in reversing the Great Migration, the southgoing blacks are repeating, with a close exactitude, a pattern in the choice of routes reminiscent of their forebears. Southern blacks who years ago joined in the Great Migration tended to adhere to what I have persuaded myself to call lanes in their progress to their promised land. The lanes, not too astonishingly, were very logical. They catered to the taking of the shortest distance between two points. There were three of them. From the Southeast, Virginia through Florida, one lane followed the Atlantic coast up to Pennsylvania and the other mid-Atlantic states, or to New England. A second lane ran from Kentucky, Tennessee, Alabama, or Mississippi to the Midwest. It fed mightily the big black ghettos in Chicago and Detroit. The Far West, the West Coast, has always actually been for blacks a portion of the North. The third lane of the Great Migration, consequently, took blacks largely from Texas, Louisiana, and Arkansas to America along the Pacific slope and particularly to California. The present reverse migration, during the three years just cited above, has brought 219,809 blacks through its eastern lane back to the Southeast. Simultaneously, only 51,083 blacks have taken this lane north. Along the far western lane, comparable figures show 186,196 blacks returning to the South and only 92,085 journeying toward the states beyond the Rocky Mountains. The midwestern lane does tell a somewhat different story. From 1985 to 1988 black migration either to the South or to the North along this lane was close to identical. Migrants going in a southerly direction totaled 183,083. Those going to the North were, in aggregate, 183,674. Not every reversing migrant, of course, has adopted the appropriate lane, just as years ago, not every black traveling in the opposite direction went where an appropriate lane would have taken him. Still, the lanes are too significant a feature of black history not to receive more than cursory recognition. They also partly explain why, in some nuances deriving from distinctions between localized black subcultures in the South, a Harlem was never quite the same black urban ghetto as a South Side in Chicago or a Watts in Los Angeles.

Further extensions of the Great Migration are, of course, to us either prophecy or more or less scientific speculation. Its essence, however, has never changed and remains to this day as it has never otherwise been, a pilgrim's progress. The pilgrim, it should go without saying, is black America. The Celestial City is a status in America acceptable to blacks. Where this status is does seem closer than it was when the Great Migration began. The great-grandchildren of the earliest migrants now are on their way in search of it. How tragic it would be should their pilgrimage last as long as that of their parents and parents' parents.

Black Exodus
The Great Migration from the American South

Dernoral Davis

Toward a Socio-Historical and Demographic Portrait of Twentieth-Century African-Americans

At the turn of this century African-Americans comprised roughly 12 percent of the nation's total population of over
75 million.[1] That 12 percent takes on particular significance when
it is remembered that throughout the post-Civil War era and late
nineteenth century there was no lack of doomsayers predicting
the numerical demise of the African-American. Indeed, among
their white contemporaries, the conventional wisdom was that
post-emancipation African-Americans were simply a doomed
race—doomed because they did not possess the ability to provide
for even their most basic needs and as a result literally would
not survive until 1900.[2]

Even the *New York Times* in 1877 joined the chorus of those
who were convinced that freedom did not agree with African-
Americans. The paper referred to an allegedly "terrific death rate"
among African-Americans and then went on to editorialize that
the causes of such mortality "need not long be sought after. They
are only too apparent to those who are conversant with the modes
of life of the Negroes of the cotton states." "They neglect or starve

their offspring," the *Times* opined, "abandon the sick to their own resources, indulge every animal passion to excess, and, when they have money, spend their nights in the most disgusting and debilitating debauches."[3]

Doomsayers even persisted into the 1890s. In 1895, Frederick Hoffman, a statistician for Prudential Insurance, reviewed and analyzed the preceding thirty years of mortality trends of African-Americans. Afterwards, he drew a set of chilling conclusions capped off by an equally dismal prognosis:

> . . . the Southern black man at the time of emancipation was healthy in body and cheerful in mind. He neither suffered inordinately from disease nor from impaired bodily vigor. His industrial capacities as a laborer were not of a low order, nor was the condition of servitude such as to produce in him morbid conditions favorable to mental disease, suicide or intemperance. What are the conditions thirty years after? The pages of this work give but one answer, an answer which is a most severe condemnation of modern attempts of superior races to lift inferior races to their own elevated position, an answer so full of meaning that it would seem criminal indifference on the part of a civilized people to ignore it. In the plain language of facts brought together, the colored race is shown to be on the downward grade, tending toward a condition in which matters will be worse than they are now. When diseases will be more destructive, vital resistance still lower, when the number of births will fall below the deaths and the gradual extinction of the race take place . . .[4]

Such accounts, many of which were widely publicized, were surely viewed as a vindication of Civil War and Reconstruction era doomsayers and undergirded a postbellum American mind set that Joel Williamson has dubbed "radical racism."[5] The very data, moreover, on which these interpreters of the black condition so confidently based their case was at best specious and its accuracy highly questionable. The nineteenth-century census data so often cited by these critics is now regarded as being notorious for its underenumeration, underreporting, and miscounting of the American populace.[6] For African-Americans the extent of these discrepancies was most pronounced.

Scholars now exhibit a keener sense of and appreciation for

the nature of the existing data. Virtually every demographer now concedes that the raw demographic data on nineteenth century African-Americans has major statistical shortcomings. Accordingly, many of these scholars, by using finely calibrated analyses and methodologies, have succeeded in adjusting for some of the intrinsic deficiencies of the data. The resulting body of findings/ estimates are less suspect and more apt to reflect actual demographic trends and patterns. Still there remains to a significant degree inconclusive and even conflicting interpretations of the African-American demographic past. Disagreement, for instance, continues to exist over the relative size of the African-American population during the nineteenth century. There is general agreement, however, that the African-American population was consistently underenumerated. The degree and magnitude of that undercount is what remains the subject of contention.

Jack Eblen and the research team of A. J. Coale and N. W. Rives have concluded in separate studies that in the nineteenth century the African-American population was underenumerated by at least 10 percent for most of the century. The African-American male was more underreported, but in 1880 both genders appear to have been about equally undercounted, while in 1890 that dubious distinction went to black females.[7] Other researchers dispute these estimates, insisting that these adjustments and revisions of the black population undercount are simply too high.[8]

A similar debate has emerged over the mortality and fertility patterns of nineteenth century African-Americans. With respect to mortality rates, the issue here again is the magnitude of the rates. Jack Eblen is convinced that while the rate of mortality remained high throughout the nineteenth century, it "improved somewhat during the last three decades of the . . ." last century. This improvement, Elben contends, has been obscured because demographers, even with their adjusted estimates of vital rates, overstated the infant and early childhood death rate, understated life expectancy (particularly among females), and consequently distorted and elevated the intrinsic rate of death.[9] Eblen, therefore, contradicts the general consensus that African-American mortality rates showed no improvement during the Civil War era and quite possibly not for the remainder of the century. If true, this would mean that

African-Americans continued to perish at the pre-Civil War level of roughly thirty deaths per thousand.

Edward Meeker has spiritedly argued, however, that there was an initial and dramatic rise in southern black mortality following the Civil War, due in large part to a sharp drop in per capita agricultural output. This per capita decline was occasioned by, according to Meeker, the vicissitudes of war and emancipation. But by 1880 returning stability and rising per capita agricultural output reduced mortality rates to their prewar levels.[10]

Estimates of life expectancy for the nineteenth century vary considerably. Both Reynolds Farley and Edward Meeker are persuaded that life expectancy of African-Americans declined over the course of the nineteenth century from the low thirties before the Civil War to the mid-twenties for both males and females after 1880. The estimates of Jack Eblen differ sharply from those of both Farley and Meeker. His figures clearly suggest that survival rates for blacks in general and females in particular improved throughout the last four decades of the nineteenth century.[11]

The nineteenth century fertility rates and patterns of African-Americans also remain the subject of a continuing debate. While most students of black fertility are sufficiently convinced that African-American reproductive rates were exceedingly high throughout most of the antebellum era then declined following the Civil War and thereafter, the reasons for and the timing of that decline is very much open to controversy. Some researchers, among them Reynolds Farley, Phillip Cutright, Edward Shorter, Clyde Kiser, and Roger Lane, point to physiological factors as the cause of declining African-American fertility.[12] In particular, they emphasized the prevalence of certain diseases, nutritional deficiencies, and generally poor health conditions within the postemancipation and late nineteenth-century African-American community. Chief among the maladies that victimized African-Americans and contributed to reduced fecundity was tuberculosis. In a recent study, Kenneth Kiple and Virginia King argued that the disease reached epidemic proportions following emancipation. They attributed the pervasiveness of tuberculosis to a diet deficient in proteins and vitamins. Some researchers have also theorized that an exceptionally high incidence of venereal diseases, especially syphilis and gonorrhea, was a factor as well in the lowering of fecundity. This conclusion rests on neither empirical nor clinical data from the last century.[13]

For his part, Eblen maintains that a decline in the black birth rate actually began a full decade prior to the Civil War, so the decline later in the century represented not a change in African-American reproductive rates but a continuation of an already prevailing trend. This trend was roughly duplicated among white Americans in the latter nineteenth century. Although for Eblen the reasons for both declines were probably similar, he only suggested that "urbanization offers an even less convincing explanation for change in black fertility than in whites."[14]

Still other researchers have emphasized socioeconomic factors over physiological ones in attempting to account for the fertility transition of the last century. Edward Meeker, for instance, using an economic conceptual framework, concluded that the decline in the black birth rate can be explained in terms of a cost-benefits analysis. In other words, as the contribution of children to their respective households declined, it made less economic sense to have large families.[15] Stewart Tolnay, in a somewhat similar analysis that focused on location-specific fertility patterns, concluded that significant differences existed between late nineteenth century rural and urban reproductive rates. These differences were linked to economic considerations involving the role and number of children within the family.[16] On the other hand, the research team of Joseph McFalls and George Masnick has emphasized the role of fertility behavior, namely birth control practices and mate exposure, in their effort to explain the post-1880 reproductive rate decline among African-Americans.[17]

Such fertility research, along with research on mortality, is of critical importance because it holds the explanatory key to patterns of black population growth during the nineteenth century. Whereas reproductive rates were relatively high until 1850, contributing to an impressive 2 to 3 percent annual rate of growth, they would later decline to less than 2 percent in the decade preceding the Civil War. It was a decline, moreover, that would break the nearly century-old pattern of the black population doubling each generation.[18] During the ensuing Civil War and Reconstruction eras, black reproductive rates apparently declined no further, at least until 1880. For the remainder of the century, the rates were down again among urban as well as rural African-Americans. This is the general consensus among scholars, although there is considerable disagreement as to the magnitude of the fertility decline and the factors and reasons that may explain it.

In other aspects of their demographic structure, namely age group, sex ratio, family and household patterns, post-emancipation African-Americans exhibited continuity and stability. Even in freedom—as in slavery—blacks remained an expectantly youthful population. More than half, 54 percent, of the postslavery and late nineteenth century African-American population was nineteen years of age and younger. Similarly, the pattern of virtual numerical sex parity of the prewar era carried over into the postwar period. For after evidencing some increased numerical disparity in 1870, the sex ratio by 1880 had returned to one of virtual parity, which continued to be the case throughout the remainder of the century.[19]

In their family and household arrangements as well, nineteenth-century African-Americans evinced both continuity and stability. Even though slaves were constantly subject to the whims of their owners, scholars are convinced that most slaves lived within single-family settings. The strongest evidence in this regard comes from plantation records and the 1860 manuscript census, which counted slave dwellings. Both sets of data indicate that slaves were invariably domiciled in single family cabins. Still more data, primarily from the Civil War era, serves to confirm this pattern of housing and family arrangement. Drawing extensively on Freedmen's Bureau marriage registers of ex-slaves, Herbert Gutman in his study of the black family found the two-parent single dwelling household the conventional, not the atypical, domestic arrangement.[20]

Gutman, along with James Smallwood, Crandall Shiffett, and Frank Furstenberg, has also convincingly demonstrated that post-emancipation African-Americans invariably organized themselves into husband-wife headed nuclear families. Indeed Gutman found that in 1880 between two-thirds and three-fourths of black children under age six lived with both parents. For that matter, in many postwar and late nineteenth century communities, the nuclear household was more prevalent among blacks than whites.[21]

Thus, by 1900, despite the many and sundry predictions of doom as well as the other circumstances that made for a precarious black existence, African-Americans were clearly not at the brink of numerical decimation. Far from having succumbed to their supposed inability to cope with freedom, African-Americans began the twentieth century collectively larger by about 4.5 million over 1860. On the strength of that increase, African-Americans numbered nearly nine million by the turn of the century. Of that number fully 90 percent, that is nearly eight million, of all African-Americans still lived in the South, where they represented about a third of the region's total population. Only a fifth of black southerners were urban dwellers, while four of five resided in the rural South. The percentage of urban dwellers varied across the South, from a high of 27 percent in Tennessee to a low of 6 percent in Mississippi.[22] As a group, however, African-Americans at this juncture were a closed population, not having been significantly impacted by in-or-out migration. That situation was to very soon change as a South-to-North migration set in, initially proceeding slowly and then at an accelerated pace.

The African-American population during the first decade of this century grew by only 10 percent and less than a million in absolute numbers. This represented a continuation of a trend that began in the closing decades of the previous century and which would remain the pattern over the ensuing three decades. By 1940, the black population had grown by an average of only 9 percent; that is, slightly more than a million per decade or at an annual rate of less than 1 percent.[23]

The explanation for such a pattern of growth is inextricably tied to the rates of total fertility and mortality for African-Americans. There is no doubt that reproductive rates fell, even plummented, during the first forty years of this century. Based on estimates made by Reynolds Farley, the fertility rate declined by at least half, from two hundred per one thousand women ages fifteen to forty-four to only one hundred. Even in their adjusted estimates, Ansley Coale and Norfleet Rives found a steady progression of birthrate declines from the late nineteenth century through the 1930s.[24]

Stanley Engerman has noted a similar pattern of decline in child/woman ratios across the entire South. When considering individual states, Engerman found that both of the Carolinas and Mississippi, which had high ratios coming out of the nineteenth century, experienced relatively small declines up to 1910. Even after 1910 this was apparently true, since child/woman ratios remained high for other southern states. Georgia and Alabama essentially followed the pattern of the Carolinas and Mississippi. Interestingly Virginia had the lowest late-nineteenth-century ratio in the South, but thereafter had only small declines in its ratio, which effectively pushed it ahead of two of the traditionally high-ratio states of Georgia and Alabama. The notable exceptions to this trend were Tennessee and Florida, which experienced fertility declines that placed them among the states with the lowest ratios.[25]

The data on location-specific child/woman ratios reveals that in southern cities, the ratios for blacks generally remained lower than that for whites between 1910 and 1940. In the rural South, too, the black child/woman ratios were generally lower. The Carolinas and Virginia, however, were the exceptions in that the decline in white child/woman ratios was steeper than that of blacks. On balance, the rural black/white ratio differential was less than that for the urban South, but by the eve of World War II black rural ratios exceeded those of whites. Over the sixty years between 1880 and 1940, the child/woman ratios of blacks and whites declined by 53 and 47 percent respectively. Furthermore, African-Americans exhibited the earliest and sharpest decline when child/woman ratios between 1880 and 1920 reached their lowest point for any census period. Conversely, the steepest decline for whites occurred between 1920 and 1940.[26]

The reasons and explanations for these patterns in southern black fertility are as unclear as the trends and configurations are clear. Some scholars have argued, mostly unconvincingly, that in the late nineteenth and early twentieth centuries, certain factors, primarily physiological ones, reduced fecundity and consequently reproductive rates. Equally unconvincing is the suggestion that the declines in general fertility and child/woman ratios were the result of changing marital and mate exposure patterns. The existing data clearly establishes that the percentage of married women with husbands present remained relatively stable. Fifty-one percent of black women aged fifteen to forty-four were so situated in 1910 and 49 percent in 1940. In fact, as late as 1940 nearly four-fifths of black households were husband-wife headed. So obviously, trends in marriage, family, and cohabitation have no explanatory utility in accounting for early twentieth century southern black fertility changes.[27]

Nor does the explanation lie in the age group or sex ratio patterns of the era. In each of these demographic structures there was continuity and stability. In the all-important twenty through forty age group, for instance, relative sex parity continued to prevail throughout the early twentieth century.[28] Even the hypothesis that systematic birth control was practiced among black women during the initial decades of this century is not supported by the data. Contraceptive studies prior to and during the Great Depression indicates that knowledge of and access to contraception was sparse. Raymond Pearl in his studies during the 1930s interviewed over five thousand urban African-American women and determined that only one in six even had attempted contraception. When Pearl contrasted reproductive rates of black women who claimed to have been users of some form of birth control with those who did not, he found no appreciable fertility difference.[29] Two later studies in the early 1940s focusing on rural and small-town black women essentially replicated the Pearl findings. Both surveys indicated that contraceptive practices were not widely used. In fact, among those women who ostensibly did practice contraception, reproduction patterns differed little from those who did not.[30]

Even Engerman's multivariable thesis that encompasses literacy, income, and urbanization fails to sufficiently explain the trends in African-American fertility previously observed.[31] Within the current body of scholarship, therefore, one finds detailed descriptions of but no convincing rationale for the black fertility decline of the early twentieth century. Essentially, what is needed is an explanation that identifies the factors or forces which triggered the fertility transition and then sustained it for more than half a century.

The assessment of early twentieth-century mortality is also difficult, primarily because of the lack of systematic death registration. Not until 1933 did all states document a minimum of 90 percent of deaths within their boundaries. Consequently, there is no definitive way to answer the critical question of whether the black death rate showed improvement during the early decades of this century. The data is simply too inconclusive. Researchers such as Farley argue that a slow and measured retrenchment in black mortality occurred prior to 1940 with the first appreciable decline taking place between 1910 and 1930. The depression years were marked by a much more significant drop as life expectancy of blacks increased. This is based on life tables fashioned from death registration statistics for 1900 and 1910 and other sources which suggest a much improved standard of living and quality of life among African-Americans in the several decades before World War II.[32]

A more pessimistic view and arguments for a later onset of declining rates of mortality are presented by Charles S. Johnson and Carter Woodson in their study of rural black southerners in the 1920s and 1930s. Both point to extremely deficient diets born of restrictions imposed on tenant farmers by landowners who feared reduced cotton acreage if food crops were allowed to be cultivated and livestock kept.[33] The prevalence of poor diets was further documented by the Department of Agriculture in a survey of 750 black rural families in the mid-1930s. That survey revealed that eight out of ten families subsisted on diets not meeting even minimum nutritional recommendations.[34]

The black South of 1940, not unlike that of forty years earlier, could still be characterized as a closed population. The initial assault on the closed population character of black southerners occurred during the World War I years. Because of out-migration, the black South lost 454,000 from its ranks, a figure roughly equivalent to the total number of departing African-Americans during the preceding forty years. On the heels of that numerical loss, the decade of the 1920s saw over 800,000 southern blacks move north. The pace of departure in the 1930s slowed to less than half that of the 1920s as some 398,000 blacks left the South.[35]

In just thirty years, then, 1.8 million black southerners left the region. Even so, the South lost for each of those three decades only between 4 and 10 percent of its native black population. This meant that in 1940, despite three decades of out-migration, nearly eight of every ten African-Americans remained a southerner by residence. But the black percentage of the total population in individual southern states and regionwide had begun to shrink. Regionally, the decline was from 30 to 24 percent between 1910 and 1940. By individual states the largest percentage declines occurred in Florida, Georgia, South Carolina, and Virginia. The smallest declines were in Alabama and Mississippi.[36]

The post-1940 demographic trends of African-Americans are less obscured and easier to study and analyze. The once-closed black population of the South would over the next four decades become decidedly more open. In the 1940s, the South suffered a loss of 1.5 million of its African-American residents, which represented a 1.5 percent drop in the region's black populace. It was the most substantial net migration loss for any single decade ever. Nevertheless, during that decade the South's black population increased by 6 percent and 543,000 in absolute numbers. The volume and pace of the exodus was basically reenacted in the 1950s, when another roughly 1.5 million black southerners absconded the region. The South's black population again showed a net increase, this time of 3 percent and 320,000 in absolute numbers for the decade. As the 1960s began, the South faced the possibility of zero growth or a net population loss among blacks for the decade, particularly if the out-migration trends of the 1940s and 1950s continued.[37]

A slight easing of the out-migration pace of the past several decades beginning in the 1960s enabled the South to avert this demographic possibility, for in the 1960s nearly a hundred thousand fewer blacks forsook the South. In a very real sense, then, the 1960s represented a pivotal demographic watershed within an already significant historical epoch. The slowing of black out-migration in the 1960s, albeit only slightly, was tantamount to a turning point, as the past two decades of migration patterns were dramatically reversed. In fact, by the early 1970s there was emerging evidence of a black remigration to the South. This early period of remigration even resulted in a net migration increase for the South; it was the first time that had happened in 30 years. By contrast, two regions of the country, the Northeast and Midwest, experienced for the first time net black migration declines while a third, the West, showed a net increase.[38]

The impact, nonetheless, of three decades of out-migration was enormous. African-Americans were by 1970 more geographically diffused across the American landscape than ever before. In general, they were both less rural and southern. Fully 80 percent of African-Americans in 1970 were urban dwellers. In the South the figure was in excess of 70 percent. This compares with less than 50 percent of all African-Americans in 1940 and about one in four black southerners. In effect, then, a dual migration had occurred with significant numbers of blacks leaving the South, one in seven, to take up residence in the Northeast, Midwest, and increasingly the West—but at the same time nonmigrating black southerners were exiting the rural South for its urban environs. And, by 1970 blacks were more urbanized than whites nationally as well as regionally.[39]

Out-migration patterns between 1940 and 1970 also had the effect of making African-Americans less geographically isolated.[40] By 1970, although a majority of African-Americans, 53 percent, still resided in the South, their numbers in other regions of the country had increased significantly. Fully one-fifth of all African-Americans resided in the Midwest, almost a fifth lived in the Northeast and about 10 percent in the West. That the South remained home to a majority of African-Americans is attributable in large measure to fertility and mortality patterns of the period. That is the first time in history that a demographic mix of rising fertility and declining mortality was present. During the 1940s and 1950s, the black birth rate rose rapidly, while in the 1940s the death rate declined appreciably. This rise/decline in birth and death rates in those two decades coincided with the largest black out-migration from the South.[41] In short, these demographic developments occurred at a time when it was possible for black southerners to absorb extensive population losses through out-migration and not be numerically decimated.

Mortality rates did not continue to fall dramatically for the whole of the post-1940 era. Nor did reproductive rates rise consistently throughout the period. After initially rising in the 1940s, mortality rates stabilized with little fluctuation over the next twenty years, 1950–1970. In general, the death rate for black men has changed only slightly in the last forty years. Black men twenty-five to forty-four years of age continue to have a mortality rate twice that of white males similarly aged.[42]

Among black women in the 1940s, there were also sharp declines in death rates across the age spectrum, but most significantly for women under thirty-five years of age. Part of the latter decline was the result of reduced deaths among young black females from a bevy of contagious diseases, including influenza, pneumonia, and tuberculosis. The maternal mortality rate fell as well from eight hundred to two hundred deaths per hundred thousand between 1940 and 1950. Over the two ensuing decades mortality rates for black women continued downward, although more slowly. By the 1970s, the rate of mortality decline among black women accelerated again with exceptionally high death rate reductions in the older age categories. Infant mortality trends for the post-1940 era have consistently been down with a more rapid pace of decline since the mid-1960s.[43]

The general downward trend in mortality among African-Americans since 1940 has served to raise life expectancy. Among males, the jump has been from fifty-two years in 1940 to roughly sixty-one in 1980, with most of this increase coming before 1950. Since the 1940s, though life expectancy for black males has increased, it has edged upward ever so slowly. Actually, the racial difference in at-birth life expectancy for men was greater in 1980 than 1950, 5.8 compared to 5.3 years. For black women, at-birth life expectancy rose from fifty-seven years in 1940 to seventy-three by 1980. The racial difference, which was ten years in 1940, had been reduced by half forty years later. Still, the life expectancy of both black males and females lagged behind the reported life spans of many western and eastern European nations as well as the more prosperous Asian cultures by four to six years.[44]

The principal causes of death among African-American males in 1950 were heart disease, stroke, influenza, homicide, and tuberculosis. More than thirty years later, deaths among black males resulting from heart disease and cerebrovascular disorders were down (though still high); other causes, however, were up, including cirrhosis, diabetes, auto accidents, suicide, and homicide. Currently, homicide is the fourth leading killer of African-American males, behind heart disease, cancer, and cerebrovascular diseases. Moreover, homicide is the primary cause of death among black men aged fifteen to thirty-four and second among males thirty-five to forty-four years of age. Similarly, black women are still as apt to die of heart disease, stroke, or some form of cancer as they were three or so decades ago. Black women also now have an increased chance of perishing in an auto accident or dying of cirrhosis and lung cancer. They have a reduced chance of being a victim of homicide or suicide.[45]

Fertility trends since 1940 initially increased rapidly, that is, up to about 1960. Thereafter fertility declined rather sharply over the next decade and a half. At its peak in 1959, the net reproduction rate for black women was 2,200. The birth rate for married black women in the post-1940 era reached its zenith around 1960 when the rate was 714 births per 1000 females. It has since fallen markedly, first to 533 and then to 322 in 1970 and 1984 respectively. The total fertility rate for black women (which is the total number of children a woman will give birth to during her lifetime) was 2.9 in 1940 as compared to 2.2 in 1984. The rate for white women in 1940 was 2.2 and forty years later 1.7. The racial difference was an average of 0.5 child—half an offspring.[46]

Clearly, the most significant demographic changes for African-Americans have been in the areas of sex ratios, marital status, and consequently family and household patterns. Indeed, the changes wrought by these population processes have served to fundamentally alter vital aspects of the African-American socio-demographic structure. Sex ratio patterns, for instance, have been moving toward increasing disparity since 1940, reversing a nearly century-old pattern of virtual numerical sex parity. Indeed, by the

1980's the sex ratio in the all-important 20–49 age range was 105 females per 100 males. Among blacks in their early twenties, the ratio was 103 females per 100 males; for those in their early thirties, 104 females, and for African-Americans aged 45–49, 106 females.[47]

These sex ratio trends, not surprisingly, have had a significant impact on marital status patterns. Perhaps the most telling of the recent data in this regard is that by 1984 a mere one in four of black women aged fifteen to forty-four lived with a spouse. That represents a decline of roughly half from twenty years earlier when some 52 percent of women so aged were residentially domiciled with their husbands. For all black women, the picture improves only slightly, to one in three.[48]

The African-American family has been impacted by these and related trends. Recent data reveals that only two in five African-American households are of the nuclear family configuration while 63, 58 and 61 percent of white, Hispanic, and Asian households were so structured. Concomitantly the percentage of female-headed households has risen dramatically since 1940 and as of 1980 comprised slightly more than one in four of all black families. This rise is significant for several reasons. The most significant is that a majority of black children are reared in female-headed households. In 1980, roughly 60 percent of black children lived in single-parent, female-headed households.[49]

Nor is it without significance that the annual income of single-parent, female-headed households is invariably and decidedly lower than that of two-parent husband-wife headed households. Figures for 1980 indicate that the average annual income of black female-headed households was under $15,000. By contrast, dual-parent husband-wife headed households had annual incomes that generally exceeded $15,000. However, fewer than one in ten black children, a mere 6 percent, lived in households in which the annual income was more than $35,000.[50]

Unquestionably, then, what this means is that a majority of black youths are growing up in households that are either at or below the poverty threshold. It is impossible, of course, to know precisely how living in such economically disadvantaged conditions will impact these black youths. If existing research is any indication, these youths will likely achieve less and fail to realize their full potential. That being the case, there will be a myriad of consequences for not only these individuals and the African-American community, but for American society at large as these throngs of less fortunate Americans are added to the ranks of a growing underclass, an underclass that has, in a very real sense, become the other America.[51]

1. In absolute terms this 12 percent translated into almost nine million African-Americans according to the census count. U.S., Bureau of the Census, *Historical Statistics of the United States: Colonial Times to 1957* (Washington: Government Printing Office, 1960) Series A 95–122; Current Population Reports, "Estimates of the Population of the United States by Age, Race and Sex: July 1, 1969," Series P-25, No. 428 (August 19, 1969), Table 2.

2. W. E. B. Dubois, *Black Reconstruction in America, 1860–1880* (New York: The World Publishing Company, 1964; originally published by Harcourt, Brace and Company in 1935), pp. 139–41.

3. Quoted in Donald Henderson, *The Negro Freedman* (New York: Henry Schumen, 1952), p. 157.

4. Quoted in Joel Williamson, *The Crucible of Race* (New York: Oxford University Press, 1984), p. 122.

5. *Ibid.*, pp. 111–39.

6. Kelley, Miller, "Enumeration Errors in Negro Population," *Scientific Monthly*, Vol. 14 (February 1922), pp. 168–87; Reynolds Farley, *Growth of the Black Population* (New York: Markham Publishing Company, 1970), pp. 24–25; Frederick Olmsted, *A Journey in the Seaboard Slave States* (New York: G.P. Putnam's Sons, 1904), II, p. 150; Francis Walker, "Statistics of the Colored Race in the United States," *Publications of the American Statistical Association*, Vol. 2 (September–December, 1890), p. 97.

7. Jack E. Eblen, "New Estimates of the Vital Rates of the United States Black Population During the Nineteenth Century," *Demography* Vol. 11 (May 1974), pp. 301–19; Ansley Coale and Norfleet W. Rives, "A Statistical Reconstruction of the Black Population of the United States, 1880–1970: Estimates of the True Numbers by Age and Sex, Birth Rates and Total Fertility," *Population Index*, Vol. 39, pp. 3–36.

8. Reynolds Farley, "The Demographic Rates and Social Institutions of the Nineteenth-Century Negro Population: A Stable Population Analysis," *Demography*

Vol. 2, pp. 386–98; Edward Meeker, "Mortality Trends of Southern Blacks, 1850–1910: Some Preliminary Findings," *Explorations in Economic History* Vol. 13, pp. 13–42.

9. Eblen, "Estimates of Vital Rates," pp. 311–12.

10. Meeker, "Mortality Trends of Southern Blacks," pp. 34–37.

11. *Ibid.*, pp. 22–27.

12. Reynolds Farley and Walter Allen, *The Color Line and the Quality of Life in America* (Washington: Russell Sage Foundation, 1987), pp. 20–23; Phillip Cutright and Edward Shorter, "The Effects of Health on the Completed Fertility of Nonwhite and White U.S. Women Born between 1867 and 1935," *Journal of Social History*, Vol. 13, pp. 191–217; Clyde Kiser, "Fertility Trends and Differentials Among Nonwhites in the United States," *Milbank Memorial Fund Quarterly* Vol. 46, pp. 149–97; and Roger Lane, *Roots of Violence in Black Philadelphia*, 1860–90 (Cambridge: Harvard University Press, 1986), p. 158.

13. See, for example, Farley and Allen, *The Color Line and the Quality of Life*, pp. 20–22; Kenneth Kiple and Virginia King, *Another Dimension of the Black Diaspora: Diet, Disease and Racism* (New York: Cambridge University Press, 1981), pp. 96–110; Cutright and Shorter, "The Effects of Health on the Completed Fertility," pp. 191–217.

14. Eblen, "Estimates of Vital Rates," p. 312.

15. Edward Meeker, "Freedom, Economic Opportunity and Fertility: Black Americans, 1860-1910," *Economic Inquiry*, Vol. 15 (July 1977), pp. 397–412.

16. Stewart E. Tolnay, "Family Economy and the Black American Fertility Transition," *Journal of Family History* Vol. 11, pp. 267–83. See also Tolnay's "Trends in Total and Marital Fertility for Black Americans, 1886–1899, *Demography*, Vol. 18, pp. 443–63; "Family Formation and Tenancy in the Farm South, 1900," *American Journal of Sociology*, Vol. 90, pp. 305–25; and with Avery Guest, "Children's Roles and Fertility: Late Nineteenth-Century United States," *Social Science History*, Vol. 7, pp. 355–80.

17. Joseph McFalls and George Masnick, "British Control and the Fertility of the United States Black Population, 1880 to 1980," *Journal of Family History*, Vol. 6, pp. 89–106; and McFalls, "The Impact of VD on the Fertility of the U.S. Black Population, 1880–1950," *Social Biology*, Vol. 20, pp. 2–19.

18. Farley, *Growth of the Black Population*, pp. 39–40; Allan Kulikoff, "A 'Prolifick' People: Black Population Growth in the Chesapeake Colonies, 1700–1790," *Southern Studies* Vol. 10, pp. 394–96; Melvin Zelnik, "Fertility of the American Negro in 1830 and 1850," *Population Studies* Vol. 20, pp. 77–83.

19. Eblen, "Estimates of Vital Rates," p. 304.

20. Herbert Gutman, *The Black Family in Slavery and Freedom*, 1750–1925 (New York: Vintage Books, 1977), pp. 9–16, 494–96; Herman Lantz and Lewellyn Hendrix, "Black Fertility and the Family in the 19th Century: A Re-examination of the Past," *Journal of Family History* Vol. 3, pp. 251–61; Shepard Krech, III, "Black Family Organization in the 19th Century: An Ethnological Perspective," *Journal of Interdisciplinary History*, Vol. 12, pp. 429–52.

21. Gutman, *The Black Family*, pp. 444–45; Crandall Shifflett, *Patronage and Poverty in the Tobacco South: Louisa County, Virginia, 1860–1900* (Knoxville: University of Tennessee Press, 1982); James Smallwood, "Emancipation and the Black Fam-

ily: A Case Study in Texas," *Social Science Quarterly*, Vol. 57, pp. 849–57; Frank Furstenberg *et al.*, "The Origins of the Female-Headed Black Family: The Impact of the Urban Experience," pp. 435–54 in Theodore Hershberg, *Philadelphia: Work, Space, Family and Group Experience* (New York: Oxford University Press, 1981).

22. Kelley Miller, "The City Negro," *Southern Workman*, (April 1902), pp. 217–22; Hollis R. Lynch, *The Black Urban Condition: A Documentary History, 1866–1971* (New York: Thomas Y. Crowell Company, 1973), pp. 48–49; Meeker, "Mortality Trends of Southern Blacks," pp. 30, 36.

23. Farley, *Growth of the Black Population*, p. 22.

24. *Ibid.*, pp. 56–58; Coale and Rives, "A Statistical Reconstruction," pp. 23–27.

25. Stanley Engerman, "Changes in Black Fertility, 1880–1940," pp. 126–153 in Tamara Hareven and Maris Vinoskis, *Family and Population in Nineteenth Century* (Princeton: Princeton University Press, 1978).

26. *Ibid.*, p. 132.

27. Farley, *The Color Line and the Quality of Life*, pp. 19–20.

28. Eblen, *Estimates of Vital Rates*, p. 304.

29. Raymond Pearl, "Preliminary Notes on a Cooperative Investigation of Family Limitation," *Milbank Memorial Fund Quarterly*, Vol. 11, pp. 37–59.

30. Gilbert Beebe, *Contraception and Fertility in Southern Appalachians* (Williams and Wilkins, 1942); Regine Stix, "Contraceptive Service in Three Areas, Part I," *Milbank Memorial Fund Quarterly*, Vol. 19, pp. 171–88.

31. Engerman, "Changes in Black Fertility," pp. 126–53.

32. Farley, *The Color Line and the Quality of Life*, pp. 27–30.

33. Charles Johnson, *Shadow of the Plantation* (Chicago: University of Chicago Press, 1934); Carter G. Woodson, *The Rural Negro* (New York: Russell and Russell, 1930).

34. See Gunnar Myrdal, *An American Dilemma: The Negro Problem and Modern Democracy* (New York: Harper Publisher, 1944), pp. 189–206.

35. U.S. Bureau of the Census, *The Social and Economic Status of the Black Population in the United States: An Historical View, 1790–1978* (Washington: Government Printing Office, 1978), p. 15.

36. *Ibid.*, p. 17.

37. Farley, "The Color Line and the Quality of Life," pp. 112–19; John Modell et al., "World War II in the Lives of Black Americans: Some Findings and an Interpretation"; *Journal of American History*, Vol. 76, pp. 838–48.

38. Bureau of Census, *Black Population in the U.S., 1790–1978*, p. 13.

39. Farley, *The Color Line and the Quality of Life*, pp. 134–36.

40. In point of fact, the shift in the black population while ending one historical form of geographic isolation and segregation, led nevertheless, to a new type, that of urban residential segregation.

41. Farley, *The Color Line and the Quality of Life*, pp. 112–13.

42. *Ibid.*, pp. 39–40.

43. *Ibid.*, pp. 47–52.

44. *Ibid.*, pp. 52–57.

45. *Ibid.*, pp. 41–45.

46. *Ibid.*, pp. 61–65.

47. Jeffery Passell and Gregory Robinson, "Revised Estimates of the Coverage

of the Population in the 1980 Census Based on Demographic Analysis: A Report on Work in Progress," *1984 Proceedings of the Social Statistics Section* (American Statistical Association, 1984), Table 3.

48. Bureau of the Census, *Census of Population: 1960*, PC (1)-ID, Table 176; Current Population Reports, series P-20 No. 399 (July 1985), Table 1.

49. Farley, *The Color Line and the Quality of Life*, p. 175.

50. *Ibid.*

51. Nicholas Lemann, "The Origins of the Underclass," *Atlantic Monthly*, Vol. 257 (June 1986), pp. 31–55.

Stewart E. Tolnay and E. M. Beck

Rethinking the Role of Racial Violence in the Great Migration

After decades of relative residential stability, southern blacks began migrating in striking numbers after the turn of the twentieth century. Reconstruction and Redemption saw a fair amount of short-distance movement as black tenant farmers exchanged one landlord for another in search of favorable financial arrangements. And, some blacks moved across state lines, generally toward the Southwest, in pursuit of King Cotton and the livelihood it promised. However, these population movements pale in comparison with the massive migration of southern blacks during the first half of this century. During the first ten years of the twentieth century, the South lost 170,000 blacks through net migration. The level of net out-migration increased substantially during the second decade to 450,000; and even further during the 1920s to 750,000 (U.S. Bureau of the Census, 1975:95). In addition to the South-North relocation, blacks *within* the South also were residentially mobile. For instance, the percent of southern blacks living in urban places grew from 17 percent in 1900 to 33 percent by 1930, and much of this black urbanization was due to migration.

Two general types of explanations have been offered for the increased mobility of southern blacks in the early part of this century: (1) those that stress underlying economic forces, including

regional wage differentials and expansion of employment opportunities in the North; and (2) those that stress underlying social
forces for example, educational opportunities, racial violence, and
voter disenfranchisement. The consensus of contemporary observers and modern investigators seems to be that economic dissatisfaction triggered the black exodus, especially as employment opportunities for blacks expanded in the North. Although frequently
mentioned, social factors, including racial violence, generally have
been accorded secondary status as a motive for black migration.

The objective of this essay is to lay the groundwork for a more
exhaustive examination of the role played by racial violence in
the migration of southern blacks after 1900. While this issue has
been considered previously (*e.g.*, Fligstein, 1981; Johnson, 1923),
certain weaknesses in data and conceptualization prevent those
analyses from being definitive. At the core of our objective are
three primary aims: (1) to review the social and economic environment within which the Great Migration occurred; (2) to pro-
pose a conceptual framework that describes how racial violence
and black migration were linked; and (3) to raise the possibility
of a reciprocal relationship between migration and racial violence,
that is, that violence induced migration, which in turn moderated
the level of violence.

A short history of black migration reveals that blacks were not
complete strangers to residential mobility before the turn of the
century. Indeed, one of the most noticeable benefits of emancipation was the freedman's ability to relocate. Between 1870 and
1900, many took advantage of this freedom to move to growing
urban areas in the South, or even to leave the South (Donald,
1921; Gottlieb, 1987). More common, however, were short-
distance moves within the rural South, as landless farmers sought
better remunerative arrangements with new landlords (Daniel,
1985; Mandle, 1978; Novak, 1978; Ransom and Sutch, 1977).
While most of these locally migratory farmers never ventured far
from home, others relocated to southwestern states where cotton
cultivation was expanding and opportunities were greater. Arkansas, Texas, and the Oklahoma Territory all experienced considerable in-migration of blacks between 1870 and 1900 (U.S. Bureau

of the Census, 1975:95).

After 1900 the pace of migration accelerated, and its character was transformed. Even as many blacks continued to circulate within the rural South, and to gravitate toward urban areas within the South, more and more migrants began to make the longer trek northward. To illustrate the extent, and variation, of the post-1900 migration of blacks, the figures in Table 1 report intercensal, net migration for the first three decades of the century (U.S. Bureau of the Census, 1975:95). Two groups of states are represented: (1) those of the "Cotton South", and (2) four northern states that were popular destinations for black migrants. All four southern states experienced net out-migration of blacks between 1900 and 1930. Furthermore, the general trend was toward heavier out-migration as the period progressed, especially for Georgia and South Carolina, two bulwarks of the Cotton South. Conversely, the northern states experienced net in-migration during these decades; and the pace of migration quickened over time. Although these crude figures are only suggestive, it is quite apparent that this period was characterized by a massive regional relocation of the black population.

If one looks closer at those states that were contributing most

TABLE 1.1

Black Population Changes in Selected Southern and
Northern States, 1900-1930

REGION	1900-1910	1910-1920	1920-1930
Cotton South			
South Carolina	−72,000	− 74,500	−204,300
Georgia	−16,200	− 74,700	−260,000
Alabama	−22,100	− 70,800	− 80,700
Mississippi	−30,900	−129,600	−68,800
Industrial North			
New York	35,800	63,100	172,800
Pennsylvania	32,900	82,500	101,700
Michigan	1,900	38,700	86,100
Illinois	23,500	69,800	119,300

of the black migrants, it becomes clear that rates of black out-migration *within the South* were not uniform. Some counties were characterized by extremely high out-migration, while others maintained relatively stable black populations. For example, in Georgia and South Carolina between 1920 and 1930, there was considerable internal variation in the extent of black out-migration across counties (see Tolnay and Beck, 1990). The heaviest black out-migration occurred in a swath running roughly through the middle of Georgia and South Carolina. Interestingly, this area defines the black belt as well as the area that had been dominated by a plantation cotton economy (Mandle, 1978). Such intra-state variation raises interesting questions about the causes of the differential migration. Why were blacks more likely to leave these regions of South Carolina and Georgia? Was the cotton economy particularly depressed? Were blacks subjected to more brutal treatment by whites in those areas? Did economic competition between whites and blacks restrict economic opportunity, and thereby encourage out-migration?[1]

Theoretical approaches to migration, in one fashion or another, generally describe "push" and "pull" factors to account for movement (or stability). Simply put, if the net attractiveness of a potential destination outweighs the net attractiveness of the place of origin, migration is expected to occur (*e.g.*, Lee, 1966; Ravenstein, 1885, 1889). Many contemporary accounts, written during the early part of the century, attempted to identify the primary explanations (push and pull factors) for the dramatic migration of blacks. The explanations proposed for the Great Migration can be divided, crudely, into *economic* and *social* forces.

Economic forces figured prominently in early discussions of black migration. In fact, most contemporary observers ascribed primary importance to economic factors. For example, Scroggs (1917:1040) wrote, " . . . the cause of the migration, like that of practically all great movements of peoples, is fundamentally economic." And, Scott (1920:13) observed that, "The economic motive stands among the foremost reasons for the decision of the group [blacks] to leave the South." These sentiments were also expressed by many others (*e.g.*, Donald, 1921; Kennedy, 1930;

Lewis, 1931; U.S. Department of Labor, 1919; Woodson, 1918 [1969]; Woofter, 1920).

The economic *push* factors operating on southern blacks were formidable. Since Emancipation, southern rural blacks had languished in a plantation economy that provided little hope of moving up the "agricultural ladder" but also offered few employment opportunities outside of farming (Mandle, 1978). At the bottom of a pecking order defined by class and caste, they were also caught in the vice-like grip of competing class interests that split the white community. On the one hand, southern planters and employers benefited from the availability of cheap black labor as long as it remained docile and servile. On the other hand, poor whites competed with black labor. This split-labor market generated conflict between poorer whites and blacks which often erupted in violence (Bonacich, 1972, 1975; Wilson, 1978). Further, it was in the interest of southern planters and employers to restrict alternative opportunities available to the black laboring class as well as to prevent a coalition of black and white labor. In short, the economic *advancement* of rural blacks was not in the interest of either class of whites, but their economic *subordination* served the interests of both.

Although a fortunate few were able to purchase land, most remained sharecroppers, tenant farmers, or farm laborers (Daniel, 1985; Flynn, 1983; Higgs, 1977; Mandle, 1978; Novak, 1978; Ransom and Sutch, 1977). Subject to the whims of landlords and the vagaries of cotton prices, most black farmers scratched a subsistence living from year to year and could offer no different future for their children. As this dismal economic situation for rural blacks persisted for decade upon decade, an environment conducive to out-migration was created. The situation in urban areas was little better, with most blacks laboring at poverty wages in unskilled occupations.

The chronic economic problems faced by southern blacks generally were translated into migration only when there was a promise of better conditions elsewhere. Often this "promise" was as close as a nearby plantation. For others the "promise" lay far to the southwest. However, the greatest potential developed in the industrial North as the World War I economy and restriction of European immigration created opportunities and wages that simply were unavailable to blacks in the South (Donald, 1921; Gottlieb 1987; Kennedy, 1930; Kiser, 1932 [1967]; Scroggs, 1917; U.S. Department of Labor, 1919; Woodson, 1918 [1969]; Woofter, 1920). For the first time since Emancipation, black labor was in demand outside of the agricultural South, and those opportunities were attractive enough to overwhelm the substantial obstacles to migration (Mandle, 1978).

The most thorough *empirical* examination of economic explanations for the black migration between 1900 and 1930 has been conducted by Fligstein (1981). He identifies three distinct dimensions to the economic explanation of southern migration: (1) the social relations of production and exchange; (2) the technical relations of production; and (3) capitalist development in the South. Fligstein infers a significant influence of the social relations of production and capitalist development on county-level net migration rates between 1900 and 1930. Especially important were tenure arrangements in agriculture, the intensity of cotton production, and the influence of urban areas (1981:124). According to Fligstein, these were the primary economic forces that determined movement of blacks into and out of southern counties. Fligstein's findings also indicate that black out-migration was linked to the spread of the boll weevil through the South.

Social causes of black migration were as widely acknowledged by contemporary observers as the economic forces, but they were nearly always considered to have been of secondary importance. Woofter (1920:121) enumerated many of the primary social factors in the following list: "Injustice in the courts, lynching, denial of suffrage, discrimination in public conveyances, and inequalities in educational advantage."

Early in the century, southern society was doubly stratified by class and race. Elaborate arrangements were made to guarantee that blacks occupied and recognized their inferior caste position. The passage of various "black codes" provided for separate and unequal facilities for blacks and whites (Flynn, 1983; Newby, 1965; Novak, 1978; Woodward, 1966). Restrictive voting statutes became more and more common after the turn of the century and effectively curtailed the black vote (Kousser, 1974). State legislatures allocated vastly unequal financial support for black and white schools and, still, county officials sometimes siphoned off the meager resources earmarked for blacks to support white schools (Kennedy, 1930; Myrdal, 1972; Woodson, 1930). As with the chronic economic hopelessness described earlier, these social abuses created an atmosphere conducive to out-migration.

One of the most telling indicators of the inferior social position of blacks in southern society was the level of lethal violence to which they were exposed. Lynching was a too common method of punishment for blacks who committed criminal acts, or who simply violated the rules of acceptable behavior for members of their caste. There has been much speculation that lynchings may have been instrumental in contributing to the willingness of southern blacks to leave their homes either for the North or for more peaceful locations in the South. As Scott wrote in his study of black migration during the First World War (1920:22), "Both whites and negroes in mentioning the reasons for the movement generally give lynchings as one of the most important causes and state that the fear of the mob has greatly accelerated the exodus." In the following section, we discuss more thoroughly the potential role of violent persecution in the migration of blacks—the central concern of this essay.

To adequately model the linkage between racial violence and black migration, we believe that each must be treated as both "dependent" and "independent" variables. That is, while racial violence is viewed as a potential incentive (push factor) for black migration, black migration is in turn seen as a force operating to reduce the level of violence against blacks. This is a critical dimension to the relationship between violent persecution and black migration, for a failure to consider such reciprocal influence could lead to very misleading conclusions about the effect of racial violence on black migration. The substance underlying this proposed reciprocal association is discussed below.

During the late nineteenth and early twentieth centuries, southern blacks were exposed to truly incredible levels of lethal violence, both at the hands of white mobs and within the white criminal justice system (Ayres, 1984; Shapiro, 1988; Williamson,

1984). For example, between 1882 and 1930, 1,663 blacks were victims of lynch mobs within the Cotton South alone.[2] But lynching was not the only form of lethal social control whites exercised over southern blacks. During the same period, 1,299 blacks were legally executed in the Cotton South. Of all those exposed to lethal social control in these states, roughly 90 percent were black.

By many accounts, the fear of violence terrorized southern blacks—especially those in areas where lynchings were common. A report by the U.S. Department of Labor (1919:107) concluded that, "Another of the more effective causes of the exodus, a cause that appeals to every Negro whether high or low, industrious or idle, respected or condemned, is the Negroes' insecurity from mob violence and lynchings." Several specific cases of heavy black out-migration have been linked to particular lynching incidents. For example, one section of Georgia experienced heavy out-migration following a series of horrible lynchings in 1915 and 1916. According to Woofter (U.S. Department of Labor, 1919:79), "The planters in the immediate vicinity of these lynchings attributed the movement from their places to the fact that the lynching parties had terrorized their Negroes." Another notorious lynching in Abbeville was followed by increased out-migration of blacks from that area of South Carolina (Ballard, 1984; Scott, 1920). Raper (1933) mentions other similar cases in his classic, *The Tragedy of Lynching.* Also, black migrants themselves mentioned the fear of violence as a reason for leaving their homes. For example, one migrant wrote eloquently to the *Chicago Defender* (quoted in Henri, 1975:130), "After twenty years of seeing my people lynched for any offense from spitting on a sidewalk to stealing a mule, I made up my mind that I would turn the prow of my ship toward the part of the country where the people at least made a pretense at being civilized."

Even the "civilized" institutions of southern society victimized blacks and represented a lethal threat. The legal web of Jim Crow and de jure second-class status of blacks, along with their cultural imperatives of racial hatred and inferiority, virtually guaranteed that the criminal justice system would be biased against blacks. Blacks were not afforded the same legal protection as whites and often were subject to summary trials with little access to legal defense. All too often these summary trials resulted in a death sentence and execution of the defendant. Raper (1933:19) saw little to distinguish many legal executions of blacks from death through mob violence: "It is not incorrect to call a death sentence under such circumstances a 'legal lynching.' " This conclusion was also reached by President Truman's Committee on Civil Rights (Shapiro, 1988:368).

It seems plausible that this violent atmosphere surrounding southern blacks should have contributed toward their willingness to migrate. Yet the little previous empirical work done to assess its impact on migration has revealed little support for such a relationship. Charles Johnson (1923) originally addressed this issue in his essay "How Much Is the Migration a Flight from Persecution?" According to Johnson (1923:272), "Persecution plays its part—a considerable one. But when the whole of the migration of southern Negroes is considered, this part seems to be limited." This somewhat contradictory conclusion was based on two key observations: (1) that counties with many lynchings were as likely to experience *increases* in black population, as they were to experience population losses; and (2) that county-level patterns in white migration closely paralleled those for black migration. It is difficult to know how much confidence to place in Johnson's "empirical" observations, since even he acknowledged (1923:274) that his analysis represented a "working test" based on a "rough correlation."

Fligstein (1981) has conducted a more sophisticated examination of the impact of racial persecution on black migration. Along with several other variables (see our earlier discussion), Fligstein included lynching as a predictor of black migration between 1900 and 1930. For each of the three decades, Fligstein's findings show a negative[3], though statistically insignificant, relationship between lynching and net migration. In light of these results, Fligstein concludes that lynching was *not* an important determinant of county-level black migration patterns.

Since Fligstein was not primarily interested in an examination of the role of racial violence, it is not surprising that his analysis cannot be considered definitive. First, the NAACP's inventory of lynchings (Fligstein's source) has been demonstrated to have serious weaknesses (Tolnay *et al.*, 1989). Second, Fligstein's lynching variable measured only whether a county experienced a lynching during the decade for which migration was measured. This measurement strategy overlooks the possibility that a climate of racial violence accumulated over a longer historical period. And it assumes that a single lynching had the same impact as 3, 4 or more lynchings. Third, Fligstein's analysis did not consider the possibility of a reciprocal *negative* impact of out-migration on subsequent lynchings.[4] While this possible relationship is discussed further, below, it should be noted that its existence could have attenuated the strength of the association between lynching and migration inferred by Fligstein.

Considering the plausibility of an association between racial violence and the Great Migration and the weaknesses of prior efforts to assess the strength of such an association, it seems clear that additional inquiry is definitely warranted.

Meanwhile, southern whites gradually began to realize that there were serious economic consequences from the out-migration of the black population. By the turn of the twentieth century, the southern economy had become extremely dependent upon cheap black labor. As the black exodus intensified, the economic impact of the loss of their labor began to be felt. As Henri wrote (1975:70), "As the trains and boats pulled out week after week and month after month, the South began to hurt from a loss of the black labor force, especially the Deep South." In response, southern planters and employers mounted a desperate attempt to restrict the labor hemorrhage. At first, their effort consisted of coercive measures. Migrants were intimidated, threatened, and abused. Labor agents were taxed, beaten, and lynched.

When coercive tactics proved ineffective, some southern communities turned to enticement. If blacks were migrating because they were unhappy or mistreated, then one solution was to make them feel more comfortable. In some areas, wages rose in response to the black exodus (Scott, 1920:86; Scroggs, 1917:103). In other areas local elites saw an increasing need to improve the plight of local blacks. For instance, the report by the U.S. Department of Labor (1919:32) observed,

... they see in the growing need for Negro labor so powerful an appeal to the self-interest of the white employer and the white planter as to make it possible to get an influential white group to exert itself actively to provide better schools; to insure full settlements between landlord and tenant on all plantations by the end of the year; to bring about abolition of the abuses in the courts of justice of the peace . . .

Importantly, it appears that in some cases, local white elites were even willing to appeal for a reduction in the level of violent persecution of the inferior caste. Scott noted such a trend when he wrote (1920:94), "The tendency to maltreat the negroes without cause, the custom of arresting them for petty offenses and the institution of lynching have all been somewhat checked by this change in the attitude of the southern white man towards the negro." Naturally, we would expect to find the emergence of this sentiment to have been more significant in areas that were suffering greater losses of their black population.

Our argument suggesting a reciprocal, moderating effect of black migration on racial violence to this point has focused primarily on the perspective of the southern white *elite*. However, it would be naive to believe that the South was monolithic in its response to black migration and the loss of black labor. In fact, there is good reason to suspect that reactions to the black exodus were split along class lines. Edna Bonacich's (1972, 1975) "Split Labor Market" theory of antagonistic ethnic relations provides an appropriate framework for developing this point. According to Bonacich blacks were one of three class groups represented in the southern economy—the other two being white planters and employers, and white laborers. Planters and employers were dependent upon cheap black labor, while the higher-priced white laborers were in competition with black labor. White laborers had everything to gain from the exodus of blacks from the South, but planters and employers had everything to lose, as described above.[5]

It is very unlikely that the planters and employers who suffered from the loss of black laborers and the poor marginal whites who competed with them responded similarly to black migration. While the former may have reacted to black migration with efforts to moderate grievances held by blacks against their white oppressors, the latter had little motivation to do so. The social and economic composition of the white community becomes, then, a critical factor in understanding the push forces behind the black exodus as well as the community's responses to it.

In sum, the proposed relationship between racial violence and black migration is not a simple one. Not only must we consider the reciprocal association between racial violence and migration, but we must also recognize that the social and economic forces that underlaid the separate components of that association were not invariant across communities.

In conclusion we note that previous discussions of the Great Migration have emphasized the role of economic forces driving blacks from the South and attracting them to large urban areas of the North. According to this paradigm, the exodus of blacks from the South was *primarily* the result of individuals deciding to leave a relatively stagnant economy for one which offered more opportunity for security and upward mobility. Although the oppressive social atmosphere for blacks in the South is typically acknowledged by proponents of the "Economic Model" of the Great Migration, its impact on out-migration is often minimized. Further, conventional wisdom and fragmentary empirical evidence seem to suggest that violence against southern blacks had a relatively trivial influence on decisions to migrate. While this interpretation of the Great Migration may eventually prove to be the most accurate, we believe that such an inference is still premature.

In this essay, we have argued that prior treatments of black migration have underestimated the importance of racial violence. We have proposed a conceptual model which describes a *reciprocal* relationship between black migration and racial violence against blacks during the first part of the twentieth century. That is, not only did southern blacks choose to leave areas in which they had been exposed to high levels of lethal violence, but the exodus of blacks in turn motivated southern whites to reduce the level of racial violence. Moreover, we have suggested that the class interests prevailing in local areas and communities helped to determine whether ameliorative efforts were made by whites to improve the living conditions for blacks and thereby discourage additional out-migration.

The historical legitimacy of this conceptual framework was demonstrated by examining the social and economic context within which the Great Migration occurred. After Emancipation lynching was an important mechanism of social control as whites sought to keep blacks in their subservient and impoverished position in southern society. And, southern blacks obviously feared lynch mobs and their vicious attempts to impose popular justice. Many blacks responded to this fear by fleeing to less violent surroundings. Once southern blacks began to leave the region in large numbers, however, some whites realized the disruptive effect the exodus could have on the southern economy. For decades southern employers had taken for granted the availability of cheap black labor; and when it was threatened, they acted in their own self-interest to staunch the flow of black labor to the North. On the other hand, white laborers saw no economic advantage to restricting the northward flow of their black competitors.

This conceptual model provides the foundation for future examination of the linkages between southern racial violence and the Great Migration. As was mentioned earlier, previous empirical investigations have either (1) failed to adequately specify the complex relationship between these two social forces or (2) were dealing with seriously flawed data. In future work, we intend to remedy some of the most important limitations of previous work by using improved data to test the usefulness of this revised conceptual framework. Newly available data on black lynchings and executions[6] will be combined with county-level data describing the social and economic environments of individual southern counties to assess the influence of racial violence and economic conditions on black out-migration. Other social, political, demographic, and cultural factors contributing to migration (and to racial violence) will also be included in future analyses to avoid drawing inferences of spurious causation. An adequate test of the conceptual framework developed in this essay undoubtedly will require a major research initiative. However, given the potential to "rewrite" the conventional wisdom regarding the dynamics of the Great Migration, that initiative will definitely be worthwhile.

This research was partially funded by grants from the National Science Foundation [SES–8618123], and the University of Georgia Research Foundation. An expanded version of this paper appeared in the Fall, 1990 issue of *Social Science History*.

1. It is probably safe to ignore cross-county variation in the attractiveness or availability of employment opportunities in the North as a possible explanation for county-level variation in net-migration. Of course, some southern counties may have had stronger ties with northern urban areas through the prior migration of family members (e.g., Ballard, 1984).

2. Traditionally, the "Cotton States" are considered to be: Alabama, Georgia, Louisiana, Mississippi, and South Carolina.

3. A negative effect of lynching on net migration may seem to contradict our hypothesis. However, it should be recognized that a positive value of net migration means a county gained population through migration. A *negative* value implies a loss of population via migration. Thus, a negative effect of lynching on net migration actually indicates that more lynchings were associated with *out*-migration (or lower levels of in-migration).

4. These points should not be interpreted as criticisms of Fligstein's analysis, since his purpose really was not to conduct a full-fledged investigation of the association between racial persecution and migration.

5. Bloom (1987) disagrees with Bonacich's (1972) assumption that black and white laborers were in direct competition. He adopts a more traditional Marxist interpretation of the sources of racial antagonism by locating primary responsibility within the white elite.

6. In a project partially supported by the National Science Foundation (SES-8618123), we are preparing a confirmed inventory of southern lynchings and executions that occurred between 1882 and 1930. These will be the ingredients of our measures of lethal racial violence.

REFERENCES

Ayres, Edward L. 1984. *Vengeance and Justice: Crime and Punishment in the 19th-Century American South*. New York: Oxford University Press.

Ballard, Allen. 1984. *One More Day's Journey: The Story of a Family and a People*. New York: McGraw-Hill.

Bloom, Jack M. 1987. *Class, Race and the Civil Rights Movement*. Bloomington: Indiana University Press.

Bonacich, Edna. 1972. "A Theory of Ethnic Antagonism: The Split Labor Market." *American Sociological Review* 37: 547–559.

———. 1975. "Abolition, the Extension of Slavery, and the Position of Free Blacks: A Study of Split Labor Markets in the United States, 1830-1863." *American Journal of Sociology* 81: 601–628.

Daniel, Pete. 1985. *Breaking the Land: The Transformation of Cotton, Tobacco and Rice Cultures Since 1880*. Urbana: University of Illinois Press.

Donald, Henderson. 1921. "The Negro Migration of 1916–1918." *The Journal of Negro History* 6: 383–498.

Fligstein, Neil. 1981. *Going North: Migration of Blacks and Whites from the South, 1900–1950*. New York: Academic Press.

Flynn, Charles L. 1983. *White Land, Black Labor: Caste and Class in Late Nineteenth-Century Georgia.* Baton Rouge: Louisiana State University Press.

Gottlieb, Peter. 1987. *Making Their Own Way: Southern Blacks' Migration to Pittsburgh, 1916-30.* Urbana: University of Illinois Press.

Henri, Florette. 1975. *Black Migration: Movement North, 1900-1920.* Garden City: Anchor Press /Doubleday.

Higgs, Robert. 1977. *Competition and Coercion: Blacks in the American Economy. 1865-1914.* Cambridge: Cambridge University Press.

Johnson, Charles S. 1923. "How Much Is the Migration a Flight from Persecution?" *Opportunity* 1: 272-274.

Kennedy, Louise Venable. 1930. *The Negro Peasant Turns Cityward: Effects of Recent Migration to Northern Centers.* New York: Columbia University Press.

Kiser, Clyde Vernon. 1932 [1967]. *Sea Island to City: A Study of St. Helena Islanders in Harlem and Other Urban Centers.* New York: AMS Press Inc.

Kousser, J. Morgan. 1974. *The Shaping of Southern Politics: Suffrage Restriction and the Establishment of the One-Party South.* New Haven: Yale University Press.

Lee, Everett S. 1966. "A Theory of Migration," *Demography* 3: 47-57.

Lewis, Edward E. 1931. *The Mobility of the Negro: A Study in the American Labor Supply.* New York: Columbia University Press.

Mandle, Jay R. 1978. *The Roots of Black Poverty: The Southern Plantation Economy After the Civil War.* Durham: Duke University Press.

Myrdal, Gunnar. 1972. *An American Dilemma: The Negro Problem and Modern Democracy.* New York: Pantheon Books.

Newby, I. A. 1965. *Jim Crow's Defense: Anti-Negro Thought in America, 1900-1930.* Baton Rouge: Louisiana State University Press.

Novak, Daniel A. 1978. *The Wheel of Servitude: Black Forced Labor after Slavery.* Lexington: University of Kentucky Press.

Ransom, Roger L. and Richard Sutch. 1977. *One Kind of Freedom: The Economic Consequences of Emancipation.* New York: Cambridge University Press.

Raper, Arthur. 1933. *The Tragedy of Lynching.* Chapel Hill. University of North Carolina Press.

Ravenstein, E. G. 1885. "The Laws of Migration," *Journal of the Royal Statistical Society.* 48: 167-227.

————. 1889. "The Laws of Migration," *Journal of the Royal Statistical Society.* 52: 241-301.

Scott, E. J. 1920. *Negro Migration During the War.* New York: Oxford University Press.

Scroggs, W. O. 1917. "Interstate Migration of Negro Population," *Journal of Political Economy* 25: 1034-1043.

Shapiro, Herbert. 1988. *White Violence and Black Response: From Reconstruction to Montgomery.* Amherst: The University of Massachusetts Press.

Tolnay, Stewart E. and E. M. Beck. 1990. "Black Flight: Lethal Violence and the Great Migration, 1900 to 1930," *Social Science History* 14: 347-370.

————, and James L. Massey. 1989. "Black Lynchings: The Power Threat Hypothesis Revisited," *Social Forces* 67: 605-623.

U.S. Bureau of the Census. 1975. *Historical Statistics of the United States: Colonial Times to 1970.* Washington. D.C.: Government Printing Office.

U.S. Department of Labor. 1919. *Negro Migration in 1916-17.* Division of Negro Economics, Washington, D.C.: Government Printing Office.

Williamson, Joel. 1984. *The Crucible of Race: Black-White Relations in the American South Since Emancipation.* New York: Oxford University Press.

Wilson, William Julius. 1978. *The Declining Significance of Race: Blacks and Changing American Institutions.* Chicago: The University of Chicago Press.

Woodson, Carter. 1918 [1969]. *A Century of Negro Migration.* New York: Russell and Russell.

———. 1930. *The Rural Negro.* Washington, D.C.: Association for the Study of Negro Life and History.

Woodward, C. Vann. 1966. *The Strange Career of Jim Crow.* Revised Edition. New York: Oxford University Press.

Woofter, Thomas Jackson. 1920. *Negro Migration: Changes in Rural Organization and Population of the Cotton Belt.* New York: W. D. Gray.

Carole Marks

The Social and Economic Life of Southern Blacks During the Migration

Unofficially, the Great Migration began in the spring of 1916. It was the start of an unusually warm summer in the East, President Wilson was preparing for reelection, women were demonstrating for a suffrage amendment, and a nation with a passion for peace was very cautiously discussing and debating "preparedness." Hardly noticed, at first, was the tiny stream of workers that the Pennsylvania railroad company brought North to work on the rail lines. Yet their experiment precipitated one of the largest population redistributions in the country's history. At its height, people were leaving at a rate of over 16,000 per month.[1] From beginning to end, nearly one-tenth of the black population of the United States would move from the South to the North. Many concluded that it was a journey into freedom, from field to factory, as the Smithsonian exhibit suggests.

There have been many analyses of this exodus: Emmett Scott's *Negro Migration During the War*, Louise Kennedy's *The Negro Peasant Turns Cityward*, and more recently, Florette Henri's *Black Migration* and William Tuttle's *Race Riot*.[2] There are, in addition, more current works that explore migration to and from specific cities, industries, and in both limited and more expansive time frames.

The migration is most familiarly depicted as a unique historical event brought on by the concurrence of the boll weevil invasion and the war in Europe. The boll weevil, in particular, marching into Texas in 1898 and eating its way across the South from west to east, is often seen as a major contributor to the exodus. In its path, thousands of agricultural laborers were thrown off the land, and the single-crop dependency of the South was ended. The war in Europe not only halted the massive immigration of industrial workers but caused some already in the United States to return to fight for their native lands. A booming war economy without a source of cheap labor and an agricultural one with surplus workers are events too convenient to need further explanation. Yet in concentrating on these, there is neglect of the subtler economic changes that the South was facing in the time period leading up to the Great Migration. For the region at this time was on the verge of "convulsive" industrial transformation. It is to these changes that this paper is addressed.

The South at the turn of the century was undergoing rapid change. "Because of the new found stability of Redemption, northern investors had provided enough capital to industrialize, and new factories were springing up across the region. Pests and floods destroyed both the profitability of cotton and the harm of its single-crop dependency. But issues of composition, compensation, and competition of labor within the new order had yet to be resolved."[3]

Black workers, however were not in position to take advantage of the change.

After centuries of agrarian dominance, the new industrial order brought decline rather than improvement in the training of black labor. In the cities, blacks were in a fierce competition for the lowest wage, and although literacy itself was likely to become a minimum requirement for even the most unskilled job, blacks were increasingly denied educational opportunity for their children. These deleterious conditions served to spawn the mass migration of black nonagricultural workers. They were literally pushed out of the South. Ironically, by leaving, they helped to further the cause of southern economic development. Industrialization at its early stages produces fewer jobs. The migration of blacks served as a useful safety valve because it reduced the labor surplus. Industrialization at its early stages destroys the privileged position of artisans. Slavery had created black monopolies in many trades, and black artisans left in large numbers during the Great Migration. Workers in the early stages of industrialization demand political recognition. White workers sought and were given a type of political participation but one made weak by their agreement to use the ballot to support only one issue, the disenfranchisement of blacks.[4]

The South began to increase production in the 1880s, many years after its neighbors to the North. Its path to change was slow and halting. By 1920, over half of the entire population (57 percent) was still engaged in agriculture, a figure that compares to the North of 1850.[5] Most industries in the South were low-wage and low value-creating enterprises that used large supplies of unskilled labor. Only rarely did these manufacturers produce finished goods for the ultimate consumer. Observed the *Manufacturers' Record*, "Much of the manufacturing of the South is still largely a case of production of materials that are used elsewhere as materials in manufacture."[6]

The South was also an area of sharp contrasts. At the end of the Civil War, "it was the poorest region in the land. By 1880, its share of wealth in the nation was about 11 percent." This figure translated into an annual per capita income of less than $400 in the South as compared with over $1,000 in the rest of the country.[7] Yet the area had the richest reserves of any region in the United States—96 percent of the bauxite, 93 percent of the phosphate rock, 69 percent of the natural gas, and 63 percent of the petroleum.[8]

The differences between an agricultural South and the industrial North were so stark that an image of the South as an underdeveloped country is appropriate. In a distribution of the percentage of workers engaged in manufacturing, a simple measure of industrial progress, it is evident that the rates for the South are well behind those for the North in 1880 (see Table 1.1). States such as Alabama, Georgia, and Mississippi were four to five times less industrialized than the state of Vermont, ten times less than states like Massachusetts and Rhode Island. While the proportions in manufacturing doubled in some southern states between 1880 and 1900, the initial levels were so low that comparisons with the North remained dismal.

TABLE 1.1

Persons Engaged in Manufacturing and Mechanical Pursuits
as Percentage of Total Gainfully Employed
by Selective Regions, 1880–1900.

REGION	1880	1900
North East		
Rhode Island	55.4	52.2
Massachusetts	50.2	46.2
Connecticut	46.8	45.3
New Hampshire	39.8	42.1
New Jersey	38.6	39.4
Pennsylvania	30.8	32.6
Maine	28.4	29.9
Ohio	23.6	27.7
Vermont	20.3	25.2
South		
Alabama	4.2	7.8
Arkansas	4.2	6.7
Florida	8.1	14.5
Georgia	5.8	9.6
Kentucky	11.2	12.9
Louisiana	8.1	9.7
Mississippi	3.0	4.7
North Carolina	6.5	12.1
South Carolina	4.8	9.9
Tennessee	7.6	9.5
Texas	5.6	7.4
Virginia	11.6	14.1
West Virginia	12.6	14.2

Source: *Statistical Abstract of the United States (Washington, D.C.: Government Printing Office, 1932).*

But the South was not without advantage. Its abundances of raw materials were particularly attractive to the North, a region that had used up much of its once abundant supply. By the 1880s, there began to appear in southern newspapers and journals an explosion of articles about raw material extraction and manufacture. Unable to finance production through indigenous capital, manufacturers made massive appeals to outside interests.

The appeals were heard. Between 1880 and 1890, "southern cotton mills increased in number from 160 to 400; spindles from 500,000 to over 4 million, mill operative from 16,000 to over 97,000."[9] The cheaper labor of the South crippled the once prosperous New England mills and set the stage for further development.

Iron and coal industries also experienced tremendous growth during this time. Concentrated in Birmingham and Chattanooga, they brought employment and new wealth to a region that, in the 1880s, had stagnated under an industry that was "feebly organized, dispersed and antiquated." With modernization, "the production of southern pig iron increased from less than 400,000 tons in 1880 to four times that amount ten years later."[10]

The bituminous coal industry was bolstered by the development of new methods of exploration, with six million tons produced in 1880 and 26 million in 1890. Cotton seed oil mills developed in the Carolinas and in Georgia and also greatly expanded during this time. Tobacco was so transformed, writes Woodward, "that everything from the steaming of the leaf to the payment of wages" was done by machinery.[11]

But development of the South also had its penalties. The South's lack of ownership and control of its own industries created a dependent relationship throughout its economic system. Most goods were only partially produced in the South, sent North for assemblage, and returned at higher prices. This exacerbated the problem of low wages and lack of opportunity, and tales of worker sufferings were almost as numerous as were the booster campaigns for development and change.

As is typical of industrialization at its early stages, there were insufficient jobs for the number of willing workers and a fierce competition resulted. Race became an issue of some importance in this competition. Jobs had always been defined along the color line with the most "dirty work" ones reserved for blacks at the bottom.

But with new technology, many jobs were redefined and the

stigma attached to them eroded. White workers replaced blacks in the railroads, on the docks, "in well digging and in sewer building." It was even acceptable, states Simpkins, for whites to be "barbers, waiters and streetcleaners." In communities throughout the South, editorials appeared demanding that jobs be given to whites first. "Blood is thicker than water," they would write. Observed one disgruntled migrant, "The whites done taken all our men's jobs, they are street workers, scavengers, dump fillers, and everything. All white men got the jobs around the city hall that colored use to have" or more directly "back to the cotton fields, city jobs are for white folks."[12]

Skilled blacks were the first group to face displacement. At the end of the Civil War, they had outnumbered whites five to one. White workers had been slowly easing them out of these positions ever since. By 1890, black monopolies in most crafts had disappeared. By the turn of the century, the very presence of blacks in the crafts was also threatened. While black artisans had never been well compensated for their work, the fact that they faced de-skilling rather than a resistant white artisan class as in the North gave the South an advantage. Table 1.2 represents a crude division of job titles within the census category manufacturing and mechanical trades. It is evident that between 1910 and 1920 there is a large increase in blacks who hold unskilled positions. In short, artisans were disadvantaged by an oppressive combination of obsolescence, competition, and community consent.

But the fabled artisan class was not alone in this. Even the most menial of positions was taken over. In some cases, laws were passed prohibiting blacks from continuing in certain lines of employment. And in a few, employers were forced to fire lower priced black labor and replace them with higher priced white labor. Displacement was sometimes achieved by dramatic processes. In Mississippi, for example, "seven blacks were murdered, seven wounded, and one flogged because they held jobs as firemen on a division of the Illinois Central Railroad."[13] "There was progress," wrote Pete Daniel, "if measured by smokestacks spindles and editorials." Yet, he adds, "poor blacks and whites continued to be ground on a treadmill."[14]

The regional disparity in wages, a manifestation of the differing

TABLE 1.2

Proportion of Black Males in Skilled and Unskilled
Manufacturing and Mechanical Trade Positions, 1910–1920 in
Major Southern States (By Number and State)

STATE	1910	1920
Alabama	(32,604)	(56,384)
% unskilled	64%	92%
% skilled and semi-skilled	36%	8%
Arkansas	(15,718)	(22,658)
% unskilled	77%	76%
% skilled and semi-skilled	23%	24%
Florida	(25,492)	(34,688)
% unskilled	70%	70%
% skilled and semi-skilled	30%	30%
Georgia	(39,345)	(60,752)
% unskilled	48%	65%
% skilled and semi-skilled	52%	35%
Kentucky	(17,715)	(18,308)
% unskilled	61%	61%
% skilled and semi-skilled	39%	39%
Louisiana	(38,138)	(47,655)
% unskilled	72%	73%
% skilled and semi-skilled	28%	27%
Mississippi	(25,702)	(33,140)
% unskilled	74%	72%
% skilled and semi-skilled	26%	28%
North Carolina	(31,891)	(46,133)
% unskilled	67%	70%
% skilled and semi-skilled	33%	30%
Oklahoma	(6,233)	(8,081)
% unskilled	80%	76%
% skilled and semi-skilled	20%	24%
South Carolina	(34,952)	(32,587)
% unskilled	46%	62%
% skilled and semi-skilled	54%	38%
Tennessee	(21,939)	(33,623)
% unskilled	63%	75%
% skilled and semi-skilled	37%	25%

TABLE 1.2 CONTINUED

Proportion of Black Males in Skilled and Unskilled Manufacturing and Mechanical Trade Positions, 1910–1920 in Major Southern States (By Number and State)

STATE	1910	1920
Texas	(27,027)	(41,794)
% unskilled	81%	75%
% skilled and semi-skilled	19%	25%
Virginia	(39,737)	(52,109)
% unskilled	68%	64%
% skilled and semi-skilled	33%	36%
West Virginia	(4,207)	(4,932)
% unskilled	68%	64%
% skilled and semi-skilled	32%	36%

Source: *U.S. Census of the Population, 1910–1920.*

levels of development, meant that wages in the North were often higher, even though most southern workers were drawn into the lowest paying, unskilled positions. For northern employers, there was a double benefit. They could provide newcomers with higher wages and still undercut their existing workforce. In the best of times, it would have been difficult for the South to compete. At this particular time, the region's selective prosperity was surrounded by persistent poverty. Complaints about conditions in the South in general, Mississippi in particular, were frequent. Wrote one migrant from Ellisville to the *Chicago Defender*, "Wages here are so low can scarcely live. We only buy enough to keep up alive I mean the greater part of the race."[15] Another migrant from Greenville explained, "Everything is so hard here everything is so high and wages is low until we just can live."[16] And from Collins a migrant reported simply, "I am a hard working man but I can't make a living here and hardly that."[17] They were not speaking simply about hard times, but dislocations associated with such economic transformations.

Economic unrest in the South was further complicated by the boll weevil invasion. This was not because it destroyed the crop, but because in doing so it was disruptive of all labor markets within and surrounding infested areas. What occurred was not a single, continuous migration, but several simultaneous ones in which farm and plantation laborers, thrown off the land, moved into towns, often undercutting the wages of existing workers. Faced suddenly with a real decrease in earnings, town dwellers were the first to take advantage of migration inducements. This circulation of population is often ignored, with many researchers preferring instead a romantic vision of farmers laying down plows in the cotton fields and arriving some time later on Cottage Grove Avenue in Chicago.

Writing in 1917, Leavell found, on the other hand, that it was "town Negroes who left the region."[18] He argues further that "It is clear that the mere fact of a Negro's having moved out of his former home is no evidence that he had moved to a northern city."[19] And he concludes, "The westward migration into the upper delta and into Arkansas would naturally be chiefly a migration of farm labor, while in the northern movement to industrial centers they would quite as naturally form a smaller proportion, for a larger number of mechanics and town workers chose the North."[20]

Support for this assertion is borne out in many of the letters to the *Chicago Defender* from black Mississippians. From Pascagoula came a request from eight or ten middle-aged men who described themselves as "property owners and have large families." A yellow pine lumber inspector from Hattiesburg wrote that he had a job which "pay me well, but as my wife and children are anxious to come north I would try and get a job now." He promised to "furnish recommendation from some reliable saw mill firms as there is in South Mississippi."[21] A carpenter from Winona wrote simply that he wanted "to go whar I can make a support for myself and family." An experienced molder from Laurel asked for a job because "I am sick of the South."[22]

Some may suggest that migrants naturally exaggerate what they could do in the hope of securing employment. Evidence indicated, however, to the contrary that migrants were disarmingly honest about their skills. Wrote one from Pascagoula, "whilse reading over the want ad of the *Defender* I find where you wants bench molders 20—not saying I am one," he wrote, "but I am a labering man and very apt to lern anything in a short while and desires to come and give it a trile or something else I can do—any thing in common labor."[23] To reiterate the point, and emphasize the drama, Mississippi was expelling some of its most experienced labor.

The South in this moment of its economic history had too many people and too few jobs, the type of migratory pressure found in most developing societies today. Indeed Keyfitz calls this "the path of the industrial revolution" and points out that European immigration to the U.S. from the 1850s on followed just this pattern of surplus displacement. The attraction of migration for experienced, nonagricultural laborers did not preclude the exodus of rural workers, but it is important to understand how difficult it was for them to leave. This point is made particularly clear when one examines the issue of transportation costs. The conventional wisdom is that employers paid these costs, later deducting them from wages. The reason this is widely claimed is that transportation costs were relatively high. Florette Henri estimates that a relatively short trip, Norfolk to Pittsburgh, would have cost a family of six over seventy-six dollars.[24] This represents significant savings to accumulate at twenty dollars per week of average urban wages. Rural wages were even less. Even for a single individual, it would be nearly a week's total income.

Migrant testimony on this issue is very clear, however. Time after time migrants report that they paid for the trip themselves though the use of savings and the sale of household goods. One reported that he sold everything that was not nailed down; furniture, clothing, pots, and pans. The advantage went, then, to those who already had resources and logically, to those who had spent some time in a wage economy. It was not easy to get to the promised land.

But the most compelling evidence comes from census survival records constructed by Lieberson (see Table 1.3). Lieberson initially wanted to examine the impact of literacy on the North, specifically whether incoming southern, illiterate migrants had a negative impact on the North. What he found instead was a general pattern of out-migration among literate groups at rates higher during the period of the Great Migration. He concluded that one out of every six literate blacks left the South during that time, indication of a very selective migration.

Migrants were directed to specific industrial centers, industries, and jobs. Between 1910 and 1920, for example, New York experienced a 66 percent increase in its black population; Chicago a 148 percent increase; Detroit a 611 percent increase; and Philadelphia a 500 percent increase. By 1920, almost 40 percent of the black population in the North was concentrated in these four cities.

TABLE 1.3
Selective Black Migration from the South,
Grouped by Age, Sex, and Literacy, 1890–1920

DECADE AND INITIAL AGE	NET MIGRATION RATE			
	MALE		FEMALE	
	ILLITERATE	*LITERATE*	*ILLITERATE*	*LITERATE*
1890–1900				
15–24	−.01770	−.06530	−.01139	−.07191
25–34	−.01079	−.02228	−.00781	−.02023
35–44	.00941	.03483	.00504	.02866
45–54	.00317	.01012	−.00566	.05037
55+	.00225	.02669	.00061	.16043
1900–1910				
15–24	−.01355	−.06520	−.01019	−.05679
25–34	−.00465	−.01169	−.00655	−.00591
35–44	.01082	.04272	−.00295	.01838
45–54	.00619	.01179	−.00336	.03499
55+	−.00219	.02426	−.00531	.08007
1910–1920				
15–24	−.03410	−.16668	−.02225	−.12395
25–34	−.02702	−.10043	−.01655	−.06579
35–44	−.01023	−.01738	−.01415	−.05237
45–54	−.00651	−.02741	−.01512	−.06039
55+	−.00657	−.02423	−.00796	−.06072

Source: *Stanley Lieberson, "Selective Black Migration from the South: A Historical View."*

The great bulk of migrants found their way into manufacturing industries with a 40 percent increase over levels found in 1910. Gains were most dramatic in the packing houses and steel industries in Chicago. In packing houses, there were sixty-seven blacks employed in 1910 and nearly three thousand in 1920. In steel, black representation increased from 6 percent in 1910 to 17 percent in 1920.

But opportunity in the North had its price, too. Many of those who followed skilled crafts in the South were barred from them in the North by company policy, union regulations, or craft tradition where there was no union. As Scott suggests, "Vacancies for blacks in industry were made only at the bottom."[25]

The great expectations with which migrants left the South from 1916 onward were never matched by the reality of the life they found in the North. They suffered not only from bad working conditions but poor health and overcrowding. Death rates were twice as high in the black communities and the rates of infant mortality were truly staggering. Tensions erupted into violence in East St. Louis in 1917, in twenty-six other northern cities in the red summer of 1918, and finally in Chicago itself in 1919.

Even the cherished dream of voter participation had its tarnished side. William Hale Thompson, Republican mayor of Chicago, had twice been elected by overwhelming support of the black migrant community. Though he managed to antagonize many groups in Chicago, including Catholics, women, and both sides of the prohibition issue, he had passed himself off to the black community as the son of a Civil War hero and frequently delighted black audiences by referring to his opponents as crackers. In the election of 1919, in fact, when barely two thousand votes separated him from his opponent, the *Defender* claimed in its post election day editorial, "Modesty prevents us from claiming victory in an election in which every other paper in Chicago was on the other side."[26]

But in 1920, after the riots, Thompson wrote to Theodore Bilbo, governor of Mississippi, "to inquire of him if it would be possible to send some of Chicago's surplus of Mississippi migrants back home." Bilbo sent back the following reply:

Your telegram, asking how many Negroes Mississippi can absorb, received. In reply, I desire to state that we have all the room in the world for what we know as N-I-G-G-E-R-S, but none whatever for "colored ladies and gentleman." If these Negroes have been contaminated with northern social and political dreams of equality, we can not use them, nor do we want them. The Negro who understands his proper relation to the white man in this country will be gladly received by the people of Mississippi, as we are very much in need of labor.[27]

On their part, though many expressed real homesickness for the South, migrants returned in very small numbers. Some were adamant about returning. When asked by a reporter of the *Journal Survey* in 1919, one migrant replied, "Miss, if I had the money I would go South and digup my fathers' and my mothers' bones and bring them up to this country (Philadelphia) I am forty-nine years old and these six weeks I have spent here are the first weeks in my life of peace and comfort."[28]

But return migration, the triumphant return of the worker made good, is a familiar dream of labor migrants because "there is no place like home" and because they are well aware that they are pawns caught between economic systems which exploit them for profit and social systems which cast them aside like handfuls of sand. For many black Mississippians, it remained only a dream.

In conclusion, the patterns of development and change experienced in the South during this period would be replicated in peripheral societies throughout the world brought into the orbit of core society expansion. For black workers, migration seemed an obvious alternative. The North, by contrast, offered them jobs, the ballot, and educational opportunity for their children. In the past, such contrasts have been sufficient to support the argument that the North, while not a promised land, would eventually provide advancement and progress. But what they did not know was that what they saw as the end of a terrible struggle for emancipation was only another beginning, and that progress in the North would be at their expense rather than at their behest.

So then how is this Great Migration to be judged? The North profited greatly from its newfound supply of cheap labor. Migrants were grateful for the dirty work jobs set aside for them. And the South in general, Mississippi in particular, lost more than it gained in this struggle, for in casting off its orphans, it discarded not only a valuable labor supply but its most useful natural resource. That migrants, acutely aware of both their vulnerability and their exploitation, nonetheless attempted to survive in the face of so much conflict is really what is great about this migration, as it is also part of its complexity. While some succeeded, there was for many more a sense of longing and of regret that was never fully erased.

1. Carole Marks, *Farewell. We're Good and Gone* (Bloomington: Indiana University Press, 1989), p.1.

2. Emmett Scott, *Negro Migration During the War* (New York: Arno Press and New York Times, 1969), Louise Kennedy, *The Negro Peasant Turns Cityward* (New York: Columbia University Press, 1930); Florette Henri, *Black Migration* (Garden City, N.Y.: Doubleday, 1975); and William Tuttle, *Race Riot* (New York: Atheneum, 1974).

3. Marks, pp. 49–50.

4. Marks, p. 50.

5. C. Vann Woodward, *Origins of the New South: 1877–1913* (Baton Rouge: Louisiana University Press, 1951), p. 309.

6. Woodward, p. 310.

7. Woodward, p. 111.

8. Woodward, p. 9.

9. Francis Butler Simkins, *The South Old and New 1820–1947* (New York: Knopf, 1947), p. 299.

10. Simpkins, p. 242.

11. Woodward, p. 237.

12. Simkins, p. 239.

13. Marks, p. 64.

14. Pete Daniel, *In the Shadow of Slavery: Peonage in the South 1901–1969* (New York: Oxford University Press, 1972), p. 10.

15. Scott, p. 305

16. Scott, p. 453

17. Scott, p. 416.

18. R. H. Leavell. "Negro Migration from Mississippi." In *Negro Migration in 1916–1917*, edited by George Haynes, (Washington, D.C.: U.S. Department of Labor, Division of Negro Economics, Government Printing Office, 1919), p. 19.

19. Leavell, p. 18

20. Leavell, p. 19.
21. Scott, p. 311.
22. Scott, p. 453.
23. Scott, p. 321.
24. Henri, p. 66.
25. Scott, p. 114.
26. Tuttle, p. 141.
27. Henri, p. 77.
28. *The Survey*, 1919, p. 238.

James R. Grossman

Black Labor Is the Best Labor: Southern White Reactions to the Great Migration

Conventionally considered part of the history of northern urban ghettos and race relations, the Great Migration has usually been viewed from a northern vantage point, with either an institutional orientation or an emphasis on the migrants as a "social problem." Recent studies have begun to examine the movement from the perspective of the migrants, focusing on the process of adaptation and on the interaction between black southerners and various aspects of the northern industrial city.[1] This volume poses a different set of questions, asking us to consider the Great Migration as an event central to our understanding of the history of the South. The response of white southerners to the Great Migration, a response triggered by black activism and shaped by class relations and ideas about race, illuminates issues at the heart of that history.

The very decision of a black southerner to leave constituted a threat to the fiber of social and economic relations in the South. Legitimacy and order relied upon the assumption that blacks were by nature docile, dependent, and unambitious. If enlightened southerners like Edgar Gardner Murphy believed that the Negro "will accept in the white man's country the place assigned him by the white man," the Great Migration represented a refusal by one-half million black southerners to cooperate.[2] Dissatisfaction and aggression were characteristics that most white southerners preferred not to associate with "their Negroes."

Although the world view threatened by such assertive black behavior might be traced back to the paternalistic ideology avowed by antebellum slave owners, this particular image of blacks emerged most clearly at the end of Reconstruction. During the 1880s most southern whites began to abandon their obsession with black treachery during the Civil War and convinced themselves that the freedmen had been "hoodwinked by the Radicals" during Reconstruction. Blacks, as Henry Grady explained reassuringly in 1876, were "peaceable and harmless," except when inflamed by troublemakers. Nearly half a century later an article appearing in two southern journals voiced the same sentiment, reminding readers that "the Negro race is a child race" except when aroused by a "disreputable, dishonest, scoundrelly element." Many southern employers and landlords agreed, and assumed that somebody had to be stirring up local blacks, thereby causing them to leave the South. Even attempts to halt migration were undermined by the inability of many prominent white southerners to recognize blacks as active and rational participants in the historical process.[3]

Few whites, however, perceived—or at least articulated—the challenge the migration posed to their own values. Most found another threat more obvious and more immediately ominous: the loss of their labor supply. If dependency existed anywhere in the South, it was in the economic nexus linking white employer to black worker. Blacks depended on white landowners and businessmen for their survival; whites depended on blacks to work their crops, cook their meals, and perform countless other tasks usually referred to as "nigger work." The plantation, whether worked by slaves, contract labor, sharecroppers, cash renters bonded by debt, or forced labor in the form of peonage, depended on the landowner's ability to keep his work force on his land. The southern economy, Booker T. Washington recognized in 1914, was "based on the Negro and the mule."[4]

Mass migration threatened to strip the South of this labor force.

"If the Negroes go," warned the Montgomery *Advertiser*, "Where shall we get labor to take their places?"[5] The South had faced this prospect before. In the aftermath of the Civil War, some whites, certain that the freedmen would refuse to work, advocated encouraging immigrants to settle in the region. Such efforts continued until the first decade of the twentieth century, but few immigrants could be enticed to work under conditions approximating those accepted by blacks only because they had little choice. "Black labor is the best labor the South can get," concluded the Columbia, South Carolina, *State* in response to the Great Migration. "No other would work long under the same conditions."[6] Only in Texas, where planters had begun recruiting Mexican laborers to work in cotton fields at least as early as the first decade of the twentieth century, did anybody find a workable solution to the problem that vexed the South during the Great Migration. When planters in the Mississippi Delta brought in "hundreds" of Mexicans to pick cotton, disease took a heavy toll and ended the experiment. The Montgomery *Advertiser*'s recognition that "the farmers of the Black Belt of Alabama cannot get on without Negro labor" applied to much of the South.[7] Ideas about race both justified the system and permitted the degree of control it required.

The Great Migration did precipitate labor shortages. In Louisiana, a federal official found "hundreds of acres of untouched land formerly cultivated . . . scores of mules in pasture because there was no help to hitch them to the plow." Sugar and rice fields were reported by a Tuskegee agent to "have grown up in grass."[8] With black tenants renting over one-fifth of its farmland in 1910 and black wage laborers working thousands of acres more, Georgia could ill afford massive emigration; by 1923, its bankers were describing the exodus as comparable only to Sherman's march to the sea in its damage to agriculture in the state.[9]

Fears of imminent bankruptcy, however, remained overstated, if not unwarranted. At the opposite extreme, the Macon *Telegraph*, a few months before it sounded the "bankruptcy" alarm in 1916, had advocated sending some of the South's surplus black labor to conquer Mexico. There were indeed fewer laborers available by 1918, although with the supply at 75 percent of "normal" that year, the South was slightly better off than agricultural employers in the rest of the country. Reliable observers reported sufficient numbers of workers still available.[10] The problem entailed less a drastic shortage than, as one white southerner perceptively suggested, "a decline from an oversupply." Lieutenant Robert Owen, investigating the situation for the Department of War, offered an incisive explanation for the South's complaints. While the shortage was "undoubtedly acute at certain centers such as Louisiana, it is not clear how severe it is all over the south. Allowance must be made for the fact that part of the clamor may be due to employers who object to paying high living wages called for by the removal of an idle surplus population." Southern landowners and employers were accustomed to this surplus, even if it was hardly "idle"; it assured sufficient hands at picking time and facilitated the exploitation of black workers which lay at the foundation of the southern economy. White southerners did not want to lose their grip on what one Georgia cotton merchant referred to as "a very amiable peasantry."[11] Migration simultaneously threatened the ready availability of that peasantry and planted doubts as to its continued amiability.

Some white southerners, especially those less dependent on black labor, ignored the migration's threat to southern ideological assumptions and rejected the premise that the region's economy could not afford an exodus of black workers. White newspapers in Nashville and Birmingham resurrected the old plea for white immigration. The president of Atlanta's Oglethorpe University located replacements closer to home, expecting that a new demand for labor would create opportunities for poor whites. Aware that he expressed a minority perspective, he urged agriculturalists to replace the migrants with well-paid white labor. The weakness of southern farming, he argued, was a result of the inefficiency of its black workers. The USDA statistician in Montgomery, Alabama, agreed, attributing the migration itself to the inability of black farmers to cope with the boll weevil. The exodus, therefore, would increase labor efficiency on the farms by eliminating the worst farmers.[12]

Other optimists touted the mechanization and diversification which they predicted would follow in the wake of the exodus. The Vicksburg, Mississippi, *Herald* expected that once rid of "thou-

sands of Negroes," farms all over southern Mississippi would finally diversify and become more productive. P. O. Davis of Alabama Polytechnic Institute agreed that "no serious cotton shortage
but a better farming system should be one result of the exodus
of Negroes." Blacks were considered "unintelligent farmers" inca-
pable of growing anything but cotton. Their departure, especially
since it would also raise the proportion of owners to tenants,
would elevate the southern farm operator, who would be more
likely to diversify into more capital-intensive crops.[13] After years
of preaching diversification and mechanization, southern agricultural reformers hoped the migration would both enable and force
landowners to adopt more efficient techniques. But they had in-
correctly identified the impediment to innovation. Black farmers
raised mostly cotton because they were forced to by landowners
and local merchants who demanded a cash crop. Given the credit
structure and sharecropping system, nobody had much incentive
to diversify or improve agricultural land. If anything promised to
change the southern crop mix, it was the devastation and frustra-
tion wrought by the boll weevil; even that shift was only transitory
at best. Dramatic and enduring transformation would await new
forces set in motion by the Great Depression and the New Deal
in the 1930s.[14]

White optimists celebrated more than the South's imminent re-
lief from dependence on supposedly inferior black farmers. Many
envisioned the lifting of an even greater burden—"educating
and civilizing" the South's black dependents. Less paternalistically
oriented whites equally applauded the departure of "worthless"
blacks. Judge Gilbert Stephenson of Winston-Salem, North Carolina, explained that "many of these young bucks already have
criminal records and, going North, add to their bad reputations."[15]
Others, although less crude, looked forward to the North's imminent sharing of the South's racial albatross. "A more equitable
distribution of the sons of Ham," hoped the Vicksburg Herald,
"will teach the Caucasians of the northern states that wherever
there is a negro infusion, there will be a race problem."[16] Some
white southerners even contemplated the possibility that eventually all blacks would leave the South, solving the "race problem"
once and for all. Although black and white leaders ascribed this

sentiment to poor whites, who often drove blacks from their homes, it did attract others as well, especially in nonplantation districts and in some cities, where black men represented more of a threat than an economic resource. Speaking for "a growing number" of optimistic whites, the New Orleans *Times-Picayune* looked beyond the temporary labor problem and cheerfully concluded that "as the North grows blacker the South grows whiter."[17]

Most influential white southerners realized that the South could not afford to be "a white man's country" if that implied racial homogeneity rather than a power relationship. Cognizant of the role black labor occupied in the southern economy, they neither encouraged migration nor welcomed its implications. Even these individuals, however, initially remained unperturbed, certain that after a short sojourn the migrants would return home.

These expectations did not seem unreasonable to many whites. Many attributed the whole movement to "the Negro's love of travel" or "wanderlust." Others assumed that jobs in the North would become scarce, as northern employers grew dissatisfied with lazy black workers.[18] Nor would the migrants themselves be satisfied. "Happy and healthy . . . when engaged in agricultural occupations," blacks would not be able to adjust to urban tenements, argued an official at the Associated Charities of Atlanta. In October 1916, the Montgomery *Advertiser* assured its readers that Chicago's chilling winds would send the migrants scampering home "within three months." Three months later, the Birmingham *News* reported the return of migrants disappointed with conditions that could not live up to those "pictured by the wily labor agents." The *Daily Herald* of Gulfport and Biloxi, Mississippi, offered similar reassurance, pointing to evidence of "a backswing of negroes from several points, many darkies finding that the promise of high wages and social equality with white folks did not come up to expectations."[19]

Expectations aside, however, few did return. White southerners increasingly began to believe black leaders who told them that the exodus was "not a temporary migration, but a movement likely to continue for an indefinite period."[20] Few faced this future with the equanimity displayed by the New Orleans *Times-Picayune,* which although "sorry to see so many able bodied Negroes leaving this community," preferred migration to "loafing around doing nothing. . . . We fancy they will be needed hereafter, and that their places will be hard to fill. But if they cannot find work here at living wages, it is better that they should go where it is offered them. . . . It would be very selfish not to want any man, black or white to go and do the very best he can for himself and his family." Most journals preferred contradictory responses, one day chronicling the migrants' return, the next bewailing their loss and advocating measures to keep workers in the South.[21]

Either immediately or eventually, civil authorities and whites dependent on black labor sought to halt the exodus through coercion, persuasion, or some combination of the two. Repressive responses involved impediments either to the transmission of information about opportunities in the North or to departure itself. Like their antebellum forebears, who had banned abolitionist literature and had forbidden slaves to play drums or trumpets because they might be used to pass signals, white southerners during the Great Migration thought they could control communication sufficiently to prevent the spread of knowledge that threatened the labor system. The Chicago *Defender*, incessant critic of the South and cheerleader of northward migration, posed an obvious target. In Meridian, Mississippi, the chief of police ordered the newspaper confiscated from dealers. Scores of other communities took similar measures, forcing the militant "race paper" underground, able to reach its subscribers only through the mail. Nor was the *Defender* the only target. In Franklin, Mississippi, a black minister was sentenced to five months on the county farm and a four hundred dollar fine for selling the NAACP's *Crisis*.[22]

Most official efforts to maintain the relative isolation of the southern labor market were directed at a more traditional menace—the labor agent, who not only transmitted information about new opportunities but even assisted migrants. As they had in the past, southern white elites ascribed black migration from the region to the influence of outsiders. Labor agents were singled out not only as the migrants' main source of information but as the very cause of the migration itself. "The Negroes who have gone North haven't gone because of any bad treatment accorded them here," insisted the Nashville *Banner* in November 1916. "They have gone because agents in search of labor needed in the great industries of the North came South in search of labor and offered them higher wages than they were making here." The influential New Orleans *Times-Picayune* accused labor agents of "enticing away" southern labor.[23] The Tennessee Coal and Iron Company tried to convince a federal investigator that there was a plot by "agents or sub-agents of some northern conspiracy" to scare blacks into fleeing from the South.[24]

Convinced that the migration depended upon outside agitation by recruiters, white southerners thought they could hold their labor supply by expelling the agents. Anti-enticement laws dating back to 1865 were dusted off, reenacted, or tightened, and by 1917, states, counties, and municipalities had established expensive licensing procedures for outside solicitation of labor. Scores of towns, cities, and counties required agents to purchase expensive permits. Some places enjoined any outsider from recruiting workers.

Even after it became apparent that this campaign against northern recruiters had failed to slow the exodus, many white southerners persisted in blaming the movement on labor agents. As migration continued through the 1920s, such notions remained so widespread that in 1923 Georgia banker James S. Peters felt compelled to tell his colleagues that "it is useless to talk about labor agents or undertake to legislate against their activities."[25] Few whites shared Peters' view that labor agents had become insignificant. Unable to recognize "their Negroes'" ability to make independent, rational decisions of such magnitude, and unwilling to confront the exploitative and oppressive nature of southern race relations, many preferred to assign to outside influences —northern whites—the pivotal role in the decision-making process of black southerners.

Labor agents did operate effectively in the Deep South, although less as "causes" of migration than as facilitators. But most whites misunderstood the dynamics of recruitment. Their assumptions about the passive character of "the Negro" led them to believe that the agents were either whites or naive black hirelings, rather than purposeful and informed members of the local black community itself. By removing or discrediting outside influences, they thought they could sustain the fiction that black Americans were best off in the South. But by 1917 it was too late; northern employers had virtually ceased sending recruiters south. They no longer had to. Stories of labor agents' activities had circulated more widely and more rapidly than the agents themselves. Most of the labor agents still operating were blacks acting on their own initiative, organizing group travel or writing North to offer their own labor and that of others. Those who did come from the North were probably visiting home, carrying small sums from employers willing to finance the journeys of friends or relatives of the recruiter. Both whites and blacks exaggerated the importance of labor agents. For whites, the mistake led to repressive actions which only fueled discontent. For blacks, it brought hope and produced a folklore which heightened the anticipation and excitement of the moment.

Attempts to limit access to transportation accompanied the repression of communication. Landlords deprived tenants of railroad fare by refusing to gin the whole cotton crop or make timely settlements.[26] Southern railroads refused to honor prepaid tickets bought through northern carriers.[27] In Macon, Georgia, police forcibly evicted several hundred Chicago-bound blacks from the railroad station. Unsure he could continue to intimidate "surly" blacks without more firepower, the chief of police promptly requested forty rifles to augment the pistols and clubs carried by his men. Outside nearby Americus, police boarded a train and arrested fifty would-be migrants. At Summit, Mississippi, local officials simply closed the railroad ticket office and had the trains pass through without stopping. "The southern white[s] are trying very hard to keep us from the north," understated an anxious Louisianian hoping to leave as soon as possible.[28]

These efforts were not confined to the local level. Charging federal agencies with encouraging and aiding the migration in the interest of war production, southern employers lobbied senators, congressmen, the Departments of Agriculture, Labor, Commerce, Justice, and War, and the War Labor Policies Board for protection and aid.[29] There was some truth to these complaints, but mainly with regard to labor recruitment for federal munitions plants in the South, hardly a threat to the long-term labor supply in the South.[30] The United States Employment Service (USES) and its parent agency, the Department of Labor, were sharply criticized for disrupting the South's labor market. But the USES, which did assist northward migration to fill labor demand in northern war industries, could hardly have been a major factor, as it "withdrew its facilities from group migration" in the summer of 1916, continuing only to "serve individual citizens regardless of race." By June 1918, the USES director for the Southern District (southern Florida, southern Alabama, Mississippi, Louisiana, east Texas) was a Meridian, Mississippi, man who quickly announced his intention "to see that Niggers were stopped from going North."[31] There is no evidence of his effectiveness in this quest, but it is unlikely that his office succored the migration. Inactivity, however, was not sufficient; southern employers wanted federal agencies to take positive steps to keep blacks on their farms and payrolls. Secretary of Labor Wilson's refusal to interfere with "the natural right of workers to move from place to place at their own discretion" contrasted sharply with white southerners' notions of their prerogatives and needs.[32]

Planters, mill operators, and local officials could prevent individuals from leaving, but the campaign of harassment and repression did not check the migratory flow. Even where prospective migrants reported that whites had "stopped the exodus," they continued to write North asking for free passes or information about reduced rate excursions. Although sufficiently intimidated to ask the *Defender* not to print such letters, these men and women were not deterred. Coercive measures to forestall migration often reinforced black southerners' doubts about the possibility of bettering their condition in the South.[33]

Many whites, especially those who counted themselves among the "best people" of the South, recognized the limitations of explicit coercion. "We are not slaveholders," the Macon *Daily Telegraph* reminded its readers. "We do not own the Negroes; we cannot compel them to stay here. Therefore we want to keep the Negroes here."[34] To do so presumably required changes addressed to the migrants' dissatisfactions: higher wages, checks on mob violence, and better schools. Recommended methods of blunting the migratory impulse, however, involved only modification of conditions. Few whites questioned the fundamental social and economic relations that frustrated blacks' aspirations to full citizenship.[35]

The assumption that blacks preferred to remain in the South underlay many arguments for improvements that would convince them to stay. "These Negroes who are leaving the South in large numbers and others who are thinking of going do not want to go," the Montgomery *Advertiser* reassured its readers.

> They prefer to remain here. But they want something to eat and to wear. They want a brighter future held out to them; they want to be reasoned with by their landlords, and want things made plain to them in the adjustment of yearly accounts; they want to be protected against lynching and personal abuse; they want better treatment on the farms, on the common carriers, and in public places in general.

Similarly, the Atlanta *Constitution* cited lynching, low wages, and poor schools as driving away people who would "prefer to stay."[36]

Recognizing that they had to convince blacks that their lives would improve in the South, southern white reformers set agendas for change. But first they had to sell reform to other whites. Throughout 1916–17 newspapers stated and restated black dissatisfactions provoking migration: lynching, low wages, "making money at the expense of the Negro's lack of intelligence," charging unfair prices, poor housing on farms and in cities, poor schools, unfair treatment by police, lack of legal protection, and even selling liquor too freely to blacks.[37] Without calling for major attitudinal or structural shifts, prominent whites prodded their communities to make adjustments necessary to retain their labor supply.

Reformers focused especially on curbing the activities of white mobs. Lynchers and "night-riders" had long acted with impunity, with newspapers and law enforcers tending to look the other way and occasionally chiding the mob afterwards. But if "respectable citizens" continued to blame terrorism on "shiftless poor whites," some editors began taking stronger positions against racial violence. Georgia's "indifference in suppressing mob law," argued the Atlanta *Constitution,* was costing the state its "best labor." The Macon *Daily Telegraph* similarly condemned night-riding.[38]

In addition to condemning mob violence, advocates of measures intended to keep blacks in the South suggested higher wages, decent schools, and aid in creating charitable organizations.[39] Concerned white spokesmen frequently focused on the plantation system, since it was on the farms where blacks were crucial to the South's economy. Blacks were not getting a "square deal," the Albany, Georgia, *Herald* lectured its readers. The Mississippi Chamber of Commerce recommended that landlords stop cheating their tenants on the price of cotton: even "good darkeys" were easy prey for labor agents whenever they were mistreated by landlords, merchants, and courts. Editors, agricultural reformers, and business leaders spelled out the antidote to migration: pay good wages; give tenants land and free time for garden plots; build better, "though inexpensive" plantation cabins; make fair settlements. The Montgomery *Advertiser* even went so far as to condemn the South's agricultural "system," which was "wrong and so had to fail." But the reference was to the one-crop system, to the South's dependence on cotton, and its consequent inefficient use of labor.[40]

It is possible that a shift away from one-crop dependence might have stimulated a change in the South's credit structure and perhaps even in landholding relationships. But none of the proponents of diversification voiced such hopes or goals. Reforms intended to convince blacks that they were better off in the South addressed only symptoms of black dissatisfaction. Even Will W. Alexander, always in the vanguard of southern racial reform, not only agreed that "many don't really want to leave," but listed only poor schools, mob violence, threats, poor crops, and "market conditions" as repelling forces. As a remedy he ambitiously suggested better protection of prisoners, changes in labor-contract law to prevent peonage, new schools and hospitals, more public health nurses, and additional efforts in the field of agricultural extension. His was the extreme liberal position; yet while it acknowledged "widespread discouragement among southern Negroes," it excluded any proposals to revise the economic and social relations that could only perpetuate such discouragement.[41] Blacks would remain subordinate, but might not detest their position to the point where they felt obliged to leave. It is possible that Alexander did favor more sweeping measures but chose to keep his program within the limits of political possibility. No white southerner of any prominence advocated changes that addressed the fundamental concern of growing numbers of blacks: condemned to dependency and subordination, they could not significantly better their condition within the South. Few whites questioned the assumption that blacks were naturally dependent and subordinate.

In some areas, scattered reforms materialized, if only temporarily. Certain that the exodus drew its main impetus from the lure of high wages in the North, many employers chose to compete by raising wages. By summer 1917, sawmills in Hattiesburg and Laurel, Mississippi, had raised the previous year's $1.10 daily rate to $1.40–$1.75. Cotton-picking outside Greenville, Mississippi, brought $2.00 per hundred pounds in November 1917, compared with 60–75 cents a year earlier. By 1918 common labor in southern rural districts had risen in two years from $ .75–1.00 per day to $1.75–2.50. Farm wages in the South, as elsewhere in the nation, more than doubled between 1915 and 1920.[42] As in other regions, they would tumble in 1921 and remain low during the "prosperity decade." But at least during World War I, it appeared that southern farmers, along with town employers, were willing to pay to keep their black workers. As one Georgia black educator carefully reported to the NAACP in 1919, "things are not quite as bad as before the war or before migration began." Except on the farms, women seldom shared this bounty, however, as domestic wages remained stable.[43]

Most of the changes that advanced beyond the advocacy and promise stage related to plantation life. Along with increasing wages, some landowners reduced rents. With black earnings still far below northern wages, rural elites searched for other incentives that would not threaten their control. Banks in Prattville, Alabama, distributed free seed for food crops. Many landlords in Alabama's Black Belt reportedly eased their abuse of tenants. Some sections even began spending more money on black schools. An official of the Russell Sage Foundation, however, identified these educational concessions as oriented almost exclusively toward agricultural training, and he predicted migration would continue anyway.[44] He was right. The changes were designed to make blacks better tenants, rather than to offer alternatives or to ease their economic dependence on whites.

Not all whites who assumed blacks wanted to stay in the South advocated reforms; even the *Advertiser* seemed unsure of its position. Like others, it argued on occasion that blacks not only did not want to leave, but had no serious grievances outside of crop failures. The same year it enumerated reforms that would stem migration, the newspaper rejected the notion that blacks faced racial barriers in the South. Impersonal economic forces "which he cannot help and which he cannot overcome" were driving the black farmer from Alabama's Black Belt. "He is not being forced out by pressure from the white race," insisted the *Advertiser's* editors. "The relations between the two races in this section were never better." T. A. Snavely, a federal investigator touring that region, found this confidence in the existence of "perfect harmony" between the races to be widespread among whites. To those who needed proof, a white educator offered Tuskegee Principal Robert R. Moton's relations with whites as an example of black satisfaction with the status quo.[45]

These contradictory positions suggest the confusion which characterized white reaction to the migration. But the contradictions went only so far. In assuming blacks wanted to stay, whites reassured themselves of the soundness of the southern racial system. Those who recognized problems saw abuses, not structural weakness. Injustice occurred, but there was no fundamental unjustice. What inequalities did exist were acceptable to both races. Like Hugh Ellis, a white man who considered himself an outspoken liberal on racial matters and who thought that "most Negroes prefer the South as a place of abode," most whites were certain that "the average Negro" neither wanted nor expected social equality. The Houston *Post* agreed, and like the New Orleans *States*, was certain that political rights were of no concern.

Whites could not understand the dynamics of the Great Migration partly because they could not envision blacks as anything but passive participants in the historical process. Buffeted by floods, insects (among which one observer included the labor agents), and occasional mob violence, migrants were portrayed as hapless refugees.[46] In this vein, the success of smooth-tongued labor agents owned less to cogency of argument than to black gullibility. Those who acknowledged that injustices had contributed to the process did not understand or perhaps even perceive the existence of blacks' ambitions to full citizenship. Modest comfort, decent schools, and some sense of hope would presumably keep blacks in their "natural home"—the South.

These responses suggest a synthesis of ideas about race and class relations in the South. Few white southerners questioned assumptions that identified blacks as inherently suited for certain types of work and likely to behave in certain ways—as long as they were not agitated by "professional negroes," labor agents, or others who had no place in a stable southern society and economy.[47] Left alone, blacks would remain in the South and would have no cause for dissatisfaction once a few problems were cleared up. If it could be shown to prospective migrants that they could earn as much in the South as in the North and that white northerners were apt to respond antagonistically to black migration, they would stay home and continue to accept a place defined by protocols of race and by specific subordinate roles in the economy.[48]

But the Great Migration posed a threat beyond the invasion of outside agitators: it suggested that ordinary black southerners lacked the very characteristics essential to their "place" in the system as a docile, easily controllable labor force. Blacks were valued in the southern economy precisely because they were supposedly naturally docile and unambitious, and because an ideology of race had become interwoven with the legal system in such a way as to permit white landlords and employers to exercise a degree of control over black tenants and workers that was probably unequalled elsewhere in the United States. To respond meaningfully to the Great Migration's ideological as well as economic threat to the system—even to acknowledge it—would be to deny both the legitimacy and the efficacy of the assumptions about race central to southern economic and social structure, and to deny as well the legitimacy and efficacy of social relations of production that relied on an ideology of race to assure adequate control over the labor force.

Parts of this essay have appeared in James R. Grossman, *Land of Hope: Chicago, Black Southerners, and the Great Migration* (Chicago: University of Chicago Press, 1989); reprinted by permission of University of Chicago Press.

1. See, e.g., Peter Gottlieb, *Making Their Own Way: Southern Blacks' Migration to Pittsburgh, 1916–1930* (Urbana: University of Illinois Press, 1987); Grossman, *Land of Hope;* Earl Lewis, *In Their Own Interests: Race, Class, and Power in Twentieth Century Norfolk* (Berkeley: University of California Press, forthcoming, 1991). For a survey of this literature, see Joe W. Trotter, "Black Migration: A Review of the Literature," in Trotter ed., *The Great Migration in Historical Perspective: New Dimensions of Race and Class in Industrial America* (Bloomington: Indiana University Press, forthcoming, 1991).

2. Quoted in George M. Fredrickson, *The Black Image in the White Mind: The Debate on Afro-American Character and Destiny, 1817–1914* (New York: Harper and Row, 1971), 287. Howard Rabinowitz has insightfully suggested how the South dealt with the previous generation of young blacks who refused to accept their "place" in his argument that Jim Crow legislation represents "white fears generated by black resistance in word and deed at the end of the 1880s." See Rabinowitz, *Race Relations in the Urban South, 1865–1890* (New York: Oxford University Press, 1978), 333–39; the quotation is from p. 339. For a different interpretation, emphasizing the autonomous force of racism, see I. A. Newby, *Jim Crow's Defense: Anti-Negro Thought in America, 1900–1930* (Baton Rouge: Louisiana State University Press, 1965), 118–22.

3. Fredrickson, *Black Image in the White Mind*, 206–07, 285–87 (Grady quotation on p. 207); "How to Stop Migration," *Manufacturers Record*, reprinted in *American Fertilizer*, 58, no. 12 (June 16, 1923): 68; Lieutenant Ray C. Burrus to Major John B. Reynolds, June 15, 1919, Box 413, Entry 359, Records of the Service and Information Branch, U.S. Department of War, RG 165, NA; "Letter intercepted by the Postal Censorship from 'Clarisse' to M. Propper," in memo from Major J. E. Spingarn to Major Walter H. Loving, July 25, 1918, File 10218–186, Box 3191, Entry 65, Files of the Military Intelligence Division, U.S. Department of War, RG 165, NA. See other correspondence in Boxes 3189–96 for southern wartime fears regarding subversion. For two contrasting views on antebellum southern "paternalism," see Eugene Genovese, *Roll, Jordan, Roll: The World the Slaves Made* (New York: Pantheon, 1974); and James Oakes, *The Ruling Race: A History of American Slaveholders* (New York: Alfred A. Knopf, 1982).

4. Clark Wissler, "Report of the Committee on the American Negro," Hanover [N.H.] Conference, August 10–13, 1926, p. 4, Folder 1020, Box 101, Laura Spelman Rockefeller Memorial Collection (LSRM), Rockefeller Archives, Tarrytown, N.Y.; Booker T. Washington, "Rural Negro and the South," *Proceedings of the National Conference of Charities and Corrections* 41 (1914), 122. See also Jay R. Mandle, *The Roots of Black Poverty: The Southern Plantation Economy after the Civil War* (Durham: Duke University Press, 1978), 69, 75.

5. Montgomery *Advertiser*, quoted in "Negro Moving North," *Literary Digest* 53, no. 15 (October 7, 1916): 877. The *Literary Digest* noted that this was the "prevailing southern comment."

6. Columbia, S.C., *State*, quoted in Emmett J. Scott, *Negro Migration During the War* (New York: Oxford University Press, 1920), 156; Ray Stannard Baker, *Following the Color Line* (1908; reprint, New York: Harper and Row, 1964), 59–60, 268;

Bert J. Loewenberg, "Efforts of the South to Encourage Immigration, 1865–1900," *South Atlantic Quarterly* 33 (October 1934): 363–85; Rowland T. Berthoff, "Southern Attitudes toward Immigration, 1865–1914," *Journal of Southern History* 17 (August 1951): 336, 342, 355.

7. Montgomery *Advertiser*, quoted in "The Looking Glass," *Crisis* 13, no. 1 (November 1916): 23; Scott, *Negro Migration*, 154–56. On Texas and Mexican labor, see T. C. Jennings to Jesse O. Thomas, Sept. 9, 1920, "Labor" Folder, Box A-3, and George B. Terrell to Jesse O. Thomas, January 20, 1926, "Labor—Negro Migration" Folder, Box A-19, both in Records of the National Urban League, Southern Regional Office, LC; Mark Reisler, *By the Sweat of Their Brow: Mexican Immigrant Labor in the United States, 1900–1940* (Westport, Conn.: Greenwood Press, 1976), 5, 78.

8. Lieutenant Ray C. Burrus to Colonel Arthur Woods, May 3, 1919, Box 600, Entry 352, Service and Information Branch, RG 165; Albon Holsey to Robert R. Moton, June 19, 1918, Box 1, Papers of Emmett J. Scott, Special Assistant to the Secretary of War, Records of the Adjutant General's Office, U.S. Department of War, RG 407, NA.

9. Charles S. Johnson, "Greenville," 3, in folder marked "Migration Study, Mississippi Summary," Box 86, Series 6, National Urban League Records, LC (hereafter cited as "Mississippi Summary," NULR); Scott, *Negro Migration*, 3; Thomas J. Woofter, *Negro Migration: Changes in Rural Organization and Population of the Cotton Belt* (New York: W. D. Gray, 1920), 63; "Exodus Costing State $27,000,000," *Journal of the American Bankers Association* 16, no. 1 (July 1923): 52.

10. Macon *Telegraph* quoted in Scott, *Negro Migration*, 156. On labor supply, see U.S. Department of Agriculture, *Yearbook*, 1924 (Washington, D.C., 1925), 1121.

11. Alfred G. Smith, "Uncle Tom Moves Up North," *Country Gentleman* 89, no. 11 (March 15, 1924): 10; Lieutenant Robert B. Owen to Major William H. Kobbe, June 1, 1919, Box 413, Entry 359, Service and Information Branch, RG 165; [Frank B. Stubbs], "Memorandum of Southern Trip," November 3, 1923–December 5, 1923, Folder 1006, Box 99, LSRM.

12. Reprints of articles from the Nashville *Banner*, 1916, and Birmingham *Age-Herald*, December 2, 1916, Box 87, Series 6, NULR; Thornwell Jacobs, "South Benefits From Migration," *Journal of the American Bankers Association* 16, no. 3 (September 1923): 181–84; F. W. Gist, "The Migratory Habits of the Negro Under Past and Present Conditions," *Manufacturers Record* 85, no. 11 (March 13, 1924): 77–79.

13. Vicksburg *Herald*, August 19, 1916, reprint in Box 86, Series 6, NULR; P. O. Davis, "Negro Exodus and Southern Agriculture," *American Review of Reviews* 63 (October 1923), 404–07.

14. Roger L. Ransom and Richard Sutch, *One Kind of Freedom: The Economic Consequences of Emancipation* (Cambridge, Eng.: Cambridge University Press, 1977), 171–76; Gavin Wright, *Old South, New South: Revolutions in the Southern Economy Since the Civil War* (New York: Basic Books, 1986), 122; Pete Daniel, *Standing at the Crossroads: Southern Life in the Twentieth Century* (New York: Hill and Wang, 1986), 11–13; Pete Daniel, *Breaking the Land: The Transformation of Cotton, Tobacco, and Rice Cultures Since 1880* (Urbana: University of Illinois Press, 1985), 91–109, 175–83. For reformers' advocacy of diversification and mechanization, see T. A. Cunningham to Atlanta *Constitution*, November 28, 1916, and Montgomery *Adver-*

tiser, October 4, 1916, both reprinted in Box 86, Series 6, NULR; Howard L. Clark, "Growth of Negro Population in the U.S. and Trend of Migration from the South since 1860. Economic Condition the Reason Negroes are Leaving South," *Manufacturers Record* 83, no. 4 (January 25, 1923): 63; John G. Van Deusen, *The Black Man in White America* (Washington, D.C.: Associated Publishers, 1938), 39–40; C. Vann Woodward, *Origins of the New South* (Baton Rouge: Louisiana State University Press, 1951), 176, 406–12.

15. "A Southern Business Man Approves Negro Migration," *Manufacturers Record* 84, no. 1 (July 5, 1923): 79; Nashville *Banner*, 1916, reprint in Box 86, Series 6, NULR; "Negro Migration as the South Sees It," *Survey* 38, no. 19 (August 11, 1918): 428.

16. Vicksburg *Herald*, August 19, 1916, reprint in Box 86, Series 6, NULR. See also Nashville *Banner*, 1916, reprint in Box 86, Series 6, NULR; Clark, "Growth of Negro Population," 63; editorials in these issues of *Manufacturers Record*: 83, no. 4 (January 25, 1923): cover; 83, no. 6 (February 8, 1923): 59–60; 83, no. 21 (May 24, 1923): 67; 83, no. 22 (May 31, 1923): 53; 83, no. 23 (June 7, 1923): 87–88; 84, no. 1 (July 5, 1923): 79; 85, no. 16 (April 17, 1924): 68. Many blacks shared a similar optimism concerning the more equal distribution of the American black population. Charles Johnson thought it would "release the South from its fear of numerical domination of Negroes." Johnson, "Negro Migrations" [c. 1926], 22, typescript in Folder 31, Box 167, Charles Johnson Papers, Fisk University Library, Nashville.

17. John Hope to W. T. B. Williams, October 10, 1917, W. T. B. Williams Mss., Hollis Burke Frissell Library, Tuskegee Institute, Tuskegee, Ala. (I am indebted to John Vernon for providing me with a copy of this letter); *Christian Advocate*, February 22, 1917, reprint in Box 86, Series 6, NULR. *Times-Picayune* quoted in "Why the Negroes Go North," *Literary Digest* 77, no. 7 (May 19, 1923): 14. For a 1908 expression of a similar sentiment by a white educator who hoped that education would stimulate black migration to Africa, see M. L. Bonham, "Answer to the Negro Question: Education," *Education* 28 (April 1908): 507-10.

18. Charles S. Johnson, "Efforts to Check the Movement," 1, in folder marked "Migration Study, Draft (Final) Chapters 7–13, Box 86, Series 6, NULR, LC (hereafter cited as "Draft," NULR); Jackson *Daily Clarion-Ledger* quoted in Neil R. McMillen, *Dark Journey: Black Mississippians in the Age of Jim Crow* (Urbana: University of Illinois Press, 1989), 262; Scott, *Negro Migration*, 72; Clark, "Growth of Negro Population," 61; Southerner, "Exodus Without Its Canaan—But Not Without its Lessons," *Coal Age* 11 (February 10, 1917): 258; Baton Rouge *State Times*, quoted in Chicago *Whip*, November 6, 1920.

19. Boyce M. Edens, "When Labor is Cheap," *Survey* 38, no. 19 (September 8, 1917): 511; Montgomery *Advertiser*, October 4, 1916, reprint in Box 86, Series 6, NULR; Birmingham *News*, November 20, 1916; *Daily Herald* (Gulfport and Biloxi), April 28, 1917.

20. George E. Haynes, "Migration of Negroes Into Northern Cities," *Proceedings of the National Conference of Social Work* 44 (1917): 496.

21. New Orleans *Times-Picayune*, December 15, 1916, reprint in Box 86, Series 6, NULR. "The Migration," *Crisis* 14, no. 1 (May 1917): 8, discusses the reaction of southern white newspapers.

22. Johnson, "Interviews," 5, NULR; Roi Ottley, *The Lonely Warrior: The Life and Times of Robert S. Abbott* (Chicago: Henry Regnery Co., 1955), 141–46; "Mis-

sissippi Freedom," *Survey* 44, no. 6 (May 8, 1920): 199–200. See also Scott, *Negro Migration*, 72–85.

23. Nashville *Banner*, November 4, 1916, reprint in Box 86, Series 6, NULR; New Orleans *Times-Picayune*, October 1, 1916, reprint in Box 87, Series 6, NULR. The isolation of the southern labor market is examined in Wright, *Old South, New South*, 65–80. On the continuity of patterns set by the southern reaction to the Kansas Exodus, see Arvarh Strickland, "Toward the Promised Land: The Exodus to Kansas and Afterward," *Missouri Historical Review* 69, no. 4 (July 1975): 383 –87.

24. S. Cullinan to W. B. Wilson, June 26, 1917; John T. Watkins to W. B. Wilson, July 14, 1917; both in File No. 8/102, Files of the Chief Clerk, U.S. Department of Labor, RG 174, NA (hereafter cited as Files-USDL, RG 174); T. R. Snavely to James Dillard [1917], File No. 13/65, Files-USDL, RG 174. Southerners were not the only people to charge that the migration was a conspiracy on the part of a group of northern whites. Democrats in Cleveland, Chicago, three cities in southern Illinois (East St. Louis, Cairo, and Danville), and elsewhere claimed that the Republicans had "colonized" blacks so as to inflate the Republican vote in 1916; see Kenneth L. Kusmer, *A Ghetto Takes Shape: Black Cleveland, 1870–1930* (Urbana: University of Illinois Press, 1976), 176; Elliott M. Rudwick, *Race Riot at East St. Louis, July 2, 1917* (Carbondale: Southern Illinois University Press, 1964), 7–15; Chicago *Daily News*, October 17–19 and November 14, 1916; Atlanta *Constitution*, November 4, 1916; Birmingham *News*, October 4, November 3, 1916.

25. New Orleans *Item*, March 23, [1917?], Box 87, Series 6, NULR; Richard W. Edmonds, "The Negro Exodus: Will It Be Permanent," *Manufacturers Record* 85, no. 16 (April 17, 1924): 77–78; "Exodus Costing State $27,000,000," 51.

26. Reprint of letter from an anonymous Mississippi minister to William Pickens, printed in Baltimore *Afro-American*, January 26, 1919, Box 86, Series 6, NULR; Johnson, "Greenwood," 2:1, "Mississippi Summary," NULR.

27. Edward C. Niles to Warren G. Harding, June 12, 1919; John R. Shillady to Walker D. Hines, June 16, 1919; Max Thelen to Hines, June 21, 1919; Hines to Edward Chambers, July 3, 1919; W. T. Taylor to Hines, July 3, 1919; Walter White to Clyde B. Aitchison, July 27, 1920; all in File P 19-3, Box 114, File of the Director General, U.S. Railroad Administration, RG 14, Washington National Records Center, Suitland, Maryland (WNRC); National Association for the Advancement of Colored People, *Tenth Annual Report for the Year 1919* (New York: National Association for the Advancement of Colored People, 1920), 44; *Defender*, December 30, 1922; Johnson, "Jackson, Mississippi," 2, "Mississippi Summary," NULR.

28. Junius B. Wood, *The Negro in Chicago* (Chicago: Chicago Daily News, 1916), 9; Scott, *Negro Migration*, 73; *Defender*, August 26, 1916; Johnson, "General," 1, "Mississippi Summary," NULR. The quotation is from Emmett J. Scott comp., "Additional Letters of Negro Migrants of 1916–18," *Journal of Negro History* 4 (October 1919): 451. This kind of obstructionism was hardly new in the South. On the persecution of black southerners who announced plans to go to Africa, see Edwin S. Redkey, *Black Exodus: Black Nationalist and Back-to-Africa Movements, 1890–1910* (New Haven: Yale University Press, 1969), 88, 112–13; on police dispersing departing groups of blacks from train stations during a migration from Georgia to Mississippi in 1899–1900, see William F. Holmes, "Labor Agents and the Georgia Exodus, 1899–1900," *South Atlantic Quarterly* 79, no. 4 (Autumn 1980): 445–46.

29. "Resolution Adopted by Agricultural Bureau of the New Orleans Association of Commerce, May 23, 1919," Box 413, Entry 359, Service and Information Branch, RG 165; John T. Watkins to W. B. Wilson, July 14, 1917, File 8/102; "Memorandum on Exodus of Negroes From the South," [1917], File 13/65; J. S. Cullinan to W. B. Wilson, June 26, 1917, File 8/102, all in Files-USDL, RG 174; Arthur Woods to Newton Baker [April 22, 1919?], Box 600, Service and Information Branch, RG 165; William C. Fitts to War Labor Policies Board, May 18, 1918; F. R. Bissell [President of Texas Portland Cement Company] to Senator Morris Sheppard, November 7, 1918; Adams Calhoun to Felix Frankfurter, June 12, 1918, all in Box 31, WLPB, RG 1.

30. William C. Fitts to War Labor Policies Board, May 18, 1918; Memo titled "Harmful Newspaper Advertising," June 20, [1918]; Adams Calhoun to Felix Frankfurter, June 12, 1918, all in Box 31, WLPB, RG 1.

31. Johnson, "The Call of the North," 2, "Draft," NULR; U.S. Department of Labor *Reports of the Department of Labor*, 1917 (Washington, D.C.: G.P.O., 1918), 79–80; Albon Holsey to Robert R. Moton, June 19, 1918, Box 1, Scott Papers, Department of War, RG 407.

32. William B. Wilson to Newton D. Baker, July 16, 1917, File 8/102, Files-USDL, RG 174. See also Wilson to J. T. Watkins, July 17, 1917, in same file. In general the Department of Labor's files during this period indicate that the department was an exception to the Wilson administration's hostility—or indifference at best—toward blacks. Secretary Wilson and Assistant Secretary Post seem to have been especially reluctant to accede to pressures to dissolve the Division of Negro Economics and to act positively to halt the migration. On attempts to convince Chicago black veterans to return South, see folder marked "Employment of Negro Ex-Servicemen," Box 600, Entry 352, Service and Information Branch, RG 165.

33. Scott, "Additional Letters," 412; *Defender*, August 9, 1919; Johnson, "Efforts to Check the Movement," 3, "Draft," NULR. See also Scott, "Letters," 334–35.

34. Bolton Smith to George E. Haynes, September 16, 1918, File 8/102, Files-USDL, RG 174; Macon *Daily Telegraph*, quoted in "The Looking Glass," *Crisis* 12, no. 6 (October 1916): 291.

35. On the centrality of full citizenship to the motivations underlying the decisions of black southerners to migrate North, see Grossman, *Land of Hope*, 13–37, 262–63.

36. Montgomery *Advertiser* [1917?], reprinted in Box 86, Series 6, NULR; "Voice of the Press on Migration of Negroes to the North," *A.M.E. Review* 33, no. 3 (January 1917): 130; Atlanta *Constitution*, quoted in Florette Henri, *Black Migration: Movement North, 1900–1920* (Garden City: Anchor Press/Doubleday, 1975), 54; Altanta *Constitution*, quoted in New York *Age*, December 14, 1916, clipping in Arthur W. Mitchell Papers, Folder 1, Box 1, Chicago Historical Society.

37. Scott, *Negro Migration*, 154–55; "Voice of the Press on Migration of Negroes to the North," 130; "The Looking Glass," *Crisis* 13, no. 4 (February 1917): 179–81. See also articles in folder marked "Migration Study, Newspaper Extracts, 1916–1917," Box 86, Series 6, NULR; Henri, *Black Migration*, 75; Scott, *Negro Migration*, 20, 59–60; "Will the South Lose by the Negro Migration Now Underway," *Manufacturers Record* 83, no. 21 (May 24, 1923): 68.

38. NAACP, *Tenth Annual Report for 1919*, 24; Carter G. Woodson, *A Century of Negro Migration* (Washington, D.C.: Association for the Study of Negro Life and

History, 1918), 177; Atlanta *Constitution*, quoted in Ottley, *Lonely Warrior*, 164; "Current Comment," *The Freeman* 7, no. 176 (July 25, 1923): 457. See also Atlanta *Constitution*, December 14, 1916, reprint in Box 87, Series 6, NULR.

39. See New York *Age*, December 14, 1916, clipping in Folder 1, Box 1, Mitchell Papers, CHS; Homer W. Borst to George E. Haynes, June 27, 1917, Folder 10, Box 1, George Edmund Haynes Papers, Fisk; Macon *Telegraph*, n.d., quoted in "The Looking Glass," *Crisis* 12, no. 6 (October 1916): 291; Johnson, "Greenwood," 2:2–3, "Mississippi Summary," NULR.

40. Albany *Herald* quoted in "Current Comment," *Freeman* 7, no. 176 (July 25, 1923): 457; Frank Andrews to Gov. Theodore J. Bilbo, June 26, 1917, folder marked "Migration Study, Negro Migrants, Letters Fr.," Box 86, Series 6, NULR; United States Department of Labor, Division of Negro Economics, *Negro Migration in 1916–17* (Washington, D.C.: G.P.O.) 25, "The Looking Glass," *Crisis* 12, no. 6 (October 1916): 291; Montgomery *Advertiser*, October 4, 1916, reprint in Box 86, Series 6, NULR.

41. W. W. Alexander, "The Negro Migration," *The Christian Index* 103, no. 23 (June 14, 1923): 6–8.

42. USDL, *Negro Migration*, 17, 23, 25; Johnson, "Greenville," 2, "Mississippi Summary," NULR; H. A. Turner, "Labor Management on some Plantations in the Yazoo-Mississippi Delta" (1916), 2, typescript in Box 85, Series 133, Records of the Office of Farm Management, Bureau of Agricultural Economics, U.S. Department of Agriculture, RG 83, NA; Monroe Work, "Effects of the War on Southern Labor," *Southern Workman* 47, no. 8 (August 1918): 382; U.S. Department of Agriculture, *Yearbook*, 1925 (Washington, D.C.: G.P.O., 1926), 1344.

43. John Dittmer, *Black Georgia in the Progressive Era, 1900–1920* (Urbana: University of Illinois Press, 1977), 191; Johnson, "Vicksburg," 5, "Mississippi Summary," NULR.

44. *Negro Farmer and Messenger*, May 5, 1917; Glenn N. Sisk, "Negro Migration in the Alabama Black Belt, 1875–1917," *Negro History Bulletin* 17 (November 1953): 34; U.S. Bureau of Education, *Report of the Commissioner of Education*, 1919 (Washington, D.C.: G.P.O., 1920), 197; Hastings Hart, "Rising Standards in the Treatment of Negroes" [1922], 2, typescript in Folder 4, Box 6, Julius Rosenwald Papers, Regenstein Library, Univ. of Chicago.

45. *Advertiser* quoted in "The Looking Glass," *Crisis* 13, no. 4 (February 1917): 179; USDL, *Negro Migration*, 60; P. O. Davis, "Negro Exodus and Southern Agriculture," 401–04.

46. See for instance, Montgomery *News*, [1916 or 1917], reprint in Box 86, Series 6, NULR; Atlanta *Constitution*, quoted in Henri, *Black Migration*, 54; Moses, "Negro Comes North," 185–86; Rev. John M. Moore, "The Migration of the Negro from the Standpoint of the South," *Eleventh Annual Meeting of the Home Missions Council* (January 1918): 24.

47. Birmingham *News*, November 14, 1916.

48. For an insightful and penetrating study that suggests the centrality of the concept of "place" to the understanding of race and class in the South, see McMillen, *Dark Journey*.

William Cohen

The Great Migration as a Lever for Social Change

In the years from the Civil War to World War I, American blacks remained largely in the South. A few came North, but this was a trickle, not a stream. Then, in 1916–1918 there took place a massive population movement. The exact number that moved in these few years is unknown, but it is clear that in the decade 1910–1920 the North experienced a net migration gain of over half a million blacks.[1] As the migration gathered force, it raised the possibility that, by voting with their feet, ordinary black laborers might transform the South and the nation.

Certainly, however, such a change would not be easy. The migration came at a time when racism was especially strong. Blacks had been driven from southern political life, segregation was omnipresent, and every year lynching took an appalling toll. Into the early twentieth century blacks did retain a few token patronage appointments in the federal government, but with the advent of the Wilson administration, they lost even these.[2]

Then, just when even the federal government seemed to be saying, "you don't count, you are not really part of American society," the Great Migration provided graphic proof of just how much blacks did count after all. In the South, the exodus provoked a wave of worry that whites were about to lose their supply of cheap labor. Some recommended forceful measures to stop northern recruiters from luring away black workers. Others contended that the best way to stem the tide was to get rid of the worst aspects of the system and to treat blacks fairly.[3] Those whites who made such proposals did not, however, go so far as to suggest that segregation be abolished.

From the very beginning, blacks put themselves in the thick of the argument. In November 1916, the Norfolk *Journal and Guide* observed that the idea in the South had been, "Keep the Negro poor, keep him ignorant and void of any ideas, and a good laborer would always be at hand." It went on to say that the exodus would not end until the South came to see the race problem "from the Negro's viewpoint."[4] In May 1917, the militant *Atlanta Independent* editorialized: "This is our home and . . . we are not going to leave, unless we are driven by want and lack of freedom." It went on to urge whites "not to drive us away [from the South] with the scarecrow of segregation, discriminations and persecution but open the doors of the shops, of the industries and facilities for our children; because we love them as they do their children."[5]

A year later, the Toussaint L'Ouverture Branch of the Savannah Chapter of the American Red Cross urged President Wilson to help bring to justice the members of a lynch mob that murdered a black woman because she had the temerity to make "an unwise remark" about the lynching of her husband. Their appeal said, "We deplore the migratory movement of the Negro from the South, yet we cannot counsel them to remain in the light of these conditions under which we live."[6]

Events reinforced the black message. World War I brought with it total mobilization and the same government that had turned a deaf ear to pleas for racial fairness now had to convince blacks that this war concerned them too. Thus it was that the administration adopted a policy of bringing a few prominent blacks into the government to deal with race-related issues. In October 1917, Emmett J. Scott was appointed special adviser to the Secretary of War on matters relating to the interests of blacks. In April 1918, the Department of Labor appointed George E. Haynes as director of the newly created Division of Negro Economics.[7]

The events leading up to the Haynes appointment illustrate the way the policies of the government intersected with the black strategy of using the migration as a lever. The initial response of the Department of Labor to the migration is best described as lethargic, but this began to change once the nation went to war. In April 1917, the Secretary of Labor asked James H. Dillard, a leading white in the southern interracial movement, to supervise a full study of the exodus.[8]

Dillard sent out five investigators to assess the extent and causes of the migration. One of these, W. T. B. Williams, was a black graduate of Hampton Institute and Harvard University. Though it might be called tokenism today, the appointment of Williams was an important symbolic event and one that was reinforced by Dillard's final conclusions. Here Dillard insisted that all popular migrations were rooted in the desire of the migrants to improve their situation and that such movements were healthy and natural. Blacks had moved, he suggested, for the same reasons that had motivated other peoples throughout history. He went on to say that the genuine progress of the United States depended on the nation's ability to spread economic opportunity and good living conditions to all races and classes.[9]

In February 1918, at the instance of the National Urban League, Dillard met with five other leading figures who shared his concern about the situation of black labor in the United States. This "Urban League Committee" included John Shillady of the NAACP and L. Hollingsworth Wood and Eugene Kinckle Jones of the National Urban League. Also in the group were Thomas Jesse Jones of the Phelps Stokes Fund and Robert Russa Moton, the principal of the Tuskegee Institute. Only Eugene Kinckle Jones and Moton were black. The committee had been called together in the wake of the adoption at an Urban League conference on Negro labor of a resolution urging the Department of Labor to appoint one or two blacks in each of its bureaus concerned with the adjustment and distribution of Negro labor.[10]

Clearly, this committee was a body that might be able to influence the government to take such a step. At its February 12 meeting, the group drew up a formal petition urging the Secretary of Labor to appoint a Negro to the Secretary's Advisory Council and asking further that blacks be appointed "to handle the problems of colored labor" in all the divisions and bureaus of the Department. Warning that "unless wisely directed," the exodus would certainly hurt wartime productivity, the committee insisted that "too much is at stake to leave undone anything that will help win the war, however much it trenches on accustomed practices."[11] Again, blacks and their white allies were trying to use the migration as a lever in the cause of racial justice.

Within the Labor Department, the petition had the warm support of Assistant Secretary Louis F. Post, and by mid-March 1918 it was rumored that a Division of Negro Economics was about to be created within the department and that it would be headed by a black person. But who would that person be and what would he stand for? The leading candidates for the job were George E. Haynes and Giles B. Jackson. Haynes, a faculty member at Fisk University and the Educational Secretary of the National Urban League, may fairly be described as the candidate of the black and philanthropic establishments represented on the Urban League Committee.[12]

Jackson, a black attorney, was also an establishment candidate, but the establishment he represented stood for a rigid maintenance of the racial *status quo*. Writing to Woodrow Wilson's private secretary, J. E. Johnson of Richmond, described Jackson as a good party adherent "allied with that element of the colored people known as the 'ante-bellums.'" He went on to say that if it were politically necessary to "place a negro-citizen in the forefront to help in this awful war emergency, there is little else to do than for the Administration to select . . . [someone who will] be least objectionable to the white citizens of the South." Precisely because Jackson could be expected to do the bidding of men like Johnson, blacks as diverse as Emmett J. Scott and W. E. B. DuBois bitterly opposed his candidacy. DuBois called Jackson "one of the most disreputable scoundrels that the Negro race has produced," and claimed that "his life, public and private, has been a succession of scandals, and if he has not a jail record it is not because he has not deserved it."[13]

Whether such protests affected the final decision is not known, but within a short time after DuBois wrote his letter, the job went to George Haynes. Now blacks had two high level spokesmen in the executive branch: Emmett Scott in the War Department and Haynes in the Labor Department. From a symbolic point of view, the appointments were an important recognition that blacks were part of the nation.[14] Now blacks could feel that at last they had a foot in the door, now they had a chance to make the country aware of their contributions and their grievances.

Tragically, while the nation that appointed these men was eager that they succeed in their role as boosters of black war morale, that same nation was much less concerned to hear what either of them had to say about racial injustice. This became painfully evident just after the war, when the government made it clear that it had no further interest in the matter of black representation in the executive branch. In mid-1919, Congress refused to renew the appropriation of the Division of Negro Economics. With the support of the Secretary of Labor, the division limped along for another year, but for all practical purposes, its demise dates from this time.[15]

Emmett Scott's post as Special Adviser to the Secretary of War also came to an end in 1919, but that is not quite the end of the story. In March, as his position was being phased out, Scott proposed the creation of a "Bureau of Negro Affairs" under the aegis of the Council of National Defense. It would be headed by a Negro citizen who, like Scott, was familiar with the South as well as the North. Scott's letter emphasized the military contribution of black soldiers and the loyalty of the black population generally, but then turned to the volatile situation that was emerging as black soldiers returned from Europe. He said that, "for reasons which need not be enumerated at this time," some of these men were "DISINCLINED TO GO BACK TO THE SOUTHERN COMMUNITIES WHERE THEY FORMERLY LIVED" even though there was a labor shortage in the South. As well, he asserted, the Negro weeklies were "making a great deal of this and heralding it as a great exodus 'from the land of slavery and oppression.'"[16]

Scott proposed then a bureau which would deal with problems emanating from black migration and from the situation of black soldiers returning from the war. This bureau would conduct practical research designed both to "locate and to KEEP IN CLOSE TOUCH WITH THE CENTERS OF UNREST. It would also give black labor a "FULL CHANCE FOR DEVELOPMENT." The proposal was warmly and genuinely endorsed by the director of the Council of National Defense to whom it was addressed but, given the racism of the times, there was no real chance that it could have been adopted.[17] Again, migration was being used as a lever, but now the government was hardly listening.

Quite by coincidence, the Great Migration occurred just as the movement for the study of black history was taking root and the two became intertwined with one another. In late 1915 and early 1916, Carter G. Woodson and others established the Association for the Study of Negro Life and History and the *Journal of Negro History*. Woodson, the leading figure in the movement, said he wanted to publicize the record of blacks so that they "may not become a negligible factor in the thought of the world."[18]

As the migration developed, Woodson came to believe that it was "the most significant event in our history since the Civil War," and he set out to make sure it would be treated as the important historical event it was. He did this first by authoring *A Century of Negro Migration*, a work that focused more on the migrations and attempts at migration that occurred *before* World War I than on the Great Migration itself. In doing this, he was deliberately setting the stage for the fuller studies of the Great Migration that would follow. Woodson devoted a concluding chapter to the contemporary exodus recognizing that it was a process "just begun." Still, this chapter touched virtually all aspects of the movement that would interest later historians.[19]

Woodson encouraged others to study the migration, and even before his book reached the public, some black scholars were doing just this. In 1917, Emmett Scott received a grant from the Carnegie Corporation, and with it he commissioned investigatory studies by Monroe N. Work, Charles S. Johnson, and T. Thomas Fortune. World War I delayed the research, and the book did not appear until 1920. Later, both Work and Johnson would publish articles of their own on the migration. Another contemporary black who wrote about the movement was George Haynes, whose article on the subject appeared a few days after he took up his duties as director of the Division of Negro Economics.[20]

The world of Great Migration scholarship was, at this time, a very small place where everyone knew everyone else. Johnson was the research director of the Chicago Urban League even while he was working for Scott, and it was at this time that he discovered and examined "about 4,000 letters written by Negroes from all parts of the South to northern persons and agencies expressing a desire to move."[21] Some of these letters would later be edited by Scott and published by Woodson in the *Journal of Negro History*. Long before writing history "from the bottom up" became fashionable, blacks were doing it. At this time also, Haynes and Work were associate editors of the *Journal of Negro History*. James Dillard was a warm supporter of Haynes, Woodson, and of Tuskegee blacks like Scott and Work.[22]

From an interpretive standpoint, the migration writings of Woodson, Scott, Haynes, and Work were similar. While all agreed that the movement was "fundamentally economic," all sought in one way or another to convey the feeling that racial persecution was central to the exodus.[23] There was a problem here, however, for as both Woodson and Scott noted, despite many years of racial persecution, blacks had not come North in large numbers until fifty years after emancipation.[24]

Attempting to deal with the issue, Scott said that the reason the migrants had not "escaped" from the South earlier was because of the absence of jobs for blacks in the North. He said that even though the causes of the migration were economic, "its roots were entangled in the entire social system of the South."[25] What Scott said was true enough, but it also sidestepped the question of the extent to which racial persecution played a direct role in driving blacks out of the South.

In 1925, Charles Johnson tackled the question head-on when he published an economic interpretation of the migration. He concluded that as a direct cause of the migration, racial persecution was relatively unimportant. He saw migration as a natural process which arose from overpopulation and which affected both blacks and whites. He said that if racial persecution were a main cause of the migration, "the direction of Negroes during the 60 years following emancipation would have been north instead of further south." Moreover, after looking at county data for lynchings and population growth, he concluded that there was no evidence that blacks were fleeing from the places where lynching was most frequent.[26]

Still, Johnson was not denying that relationships existed between race and migration. Although he insisted that forces like overpopulation and better wages were far more significant as causes than matters like segregation and lynching, he was quick to say that because blacks were at the bottom of the economic ladder, they experienced the impersonal forces of the economy differently than whites. In particular, he attacked the plantation system as being "ill-adapted to free labor," arguing that because of it there was an "abnormal congestion of the Negro population on an area insufficient to support them."[27]

Despite his strong emphasis on the economic dimension, Johnson certainly could have accepted Scott's formulation that the roots of the migration "were entangled in the entire social system of the South." The difference between them was as much a matter of style as of substance. While a graduate student in Sociology at the University of Chicago, Johnson had been strongly influenced by Robert E. Park, who held that racial issues could and should be studied in a detached and scientific manner. Throughout his long and distinguished career as a sociologist, Johnson's work would be characterized by just such an approach.[28]

At the same time, it was also true that underlying Johnson's scientific detachment was a bedrock commitment to the principle of equality. When he casually assumed that black migration occurs for the same reasons as white migration, he was building this principle into his work as a fundamental assumption. When he wrote in such a detached manner about the drawbacks of the plantation system, the neutrality of his discussion was real enough on one level. On another level, that neutrality was itself a tool for getting white people to hear a black man's criticisms of the plantation system.[29] Thus, for Charles Johnson, too, the migration was a lever for social change.

In a time when blacks were almost powerless to affect government decisions, the Great Migration brought the possibility that they might be able to affect events after all by arguing that the migration was the outcome of southern racial oppression. If only the oppression would stop, so would the outflow of black labor. The theme appears everywhere, in editorials in black newspapers, in appeals for the President to act against lynching, and in appeals for the appointment of blacks to government posts.

It also appears in historical works about the migration, but here the matter becomes more complicated. Those who wrote such works were scholars as well as advocates. Thus, many of the works on the migration reflect a certain tension as between the economic and social causes of the migration. Often the authors of these works tried to have it both ways, conceding the centrality of economic forces but suggesting still that racial oppression was the main force behind the movement.

They were right and they were wrong. Given the lack of correlation between lynching data and population statistics, it is hard to argue that the migration was a direct flight from violent oppression. At the same time, there is no denying that the economic status of the blacks who chose to go North was the product of a southern economy suffused with racism.

1. Hope T. Eldridge and Dorothy Swaine Thomas, *Demographic Analyses and Interrelations*, Vol. III of *Population Redistribution and Economic Growth, United States, 1870–1950*, Simon Kuznets and Dorothy Swaine Thomas, gen. eds. (Philadelphia, 1964), Table 1.27 p. 90. There are no reliable figures on the number that came in 1916–1918, but virtually all observers agree that a large increase took place at this time. See, for example, U.S. Department of Labor, *Negro Migration in 1916–17, Reports by R. H. Leavell, T. R. Snavely, T. J. Woofter, Jr., W. T. B. Williams, and Francis D. Tyson* (Washington, 1919), pp. 17, 52, 97, 83, 115–117, *passim*.

2. Jane Lang Scheiber and Harry N. Scheiber, "The Wilson Administration and the Wartime Mobilization of Black Americans, 1917–18," *Labor History*, 10 (1969), 433–435.

3. Nashville *Banner*, November 4, 1916, Columbus (Ga.) *Empire-Sun*, December 2, 1916, typescript copies in National Urban League Records, series 6, box 86, Library of Congress; Natchez *Democrat*, September 30, October 2, 1917.

4. Norfolk *Journal and Guide*, November 25, 1916.

5. *Atlanta Independent*, May 26, 1917, typescript copy in Carter G. Woodson Collection, Migration Papers, box 11, folder 148, Library of Congress.

6. Rebecca Stiles Wilson and Mary E. Belcher to Wilson, May 31, 1918, file 158260, no. 55, Department of Justice, Straight Numerical File, National Archives, Record Group 60.

7. Emmett J. Scott, *Scott's Official History of the American Negro in the World War* (Chicago: Homewood Press, 1919), pp. 40–41; William B. Wilson to George E. Haynes, April 18, 1918, General Records of the Department of Labor, File

8–102A, National Archives, Record Group 174. Hereafter cited in the form: Labor Department, file 8–102A.

8. U.S. Department of Labor, *Fifth Annual Report of the Secretary of Labor* (Washington, D. C., 1917), pp. 77–78; August Meier and Elliot Rudwick, *Black History and the Historical Profession* (Urbana: University of Illinois Press, 1986), p. 16.

9. Department of Labor, *Negro Migration*, pp. 5, 9–13. Dillard wrote his introduction in April 1918.

10. John D. Finney, "A Study of Negro Labor During and After World War I" (Ph.D. dissertation, Georgetown University, 1967), pp. 124–127; Nancy J. Weiss, *The National Urban League, 1910–1940* (New York: Oxford University Press, 1974), pp. 133–134.

11. Robert R. Moton, James H. Dillard, L. Hollingsworth Wood, Eugene K. Jones, John Shillady, Thomas J. Jones to William B. Wilson, February 12, 1918, Labor Department, file 8–102F.

12. Finney, "Negro Labor," pp. 150–153; Meier and Rudwick, *Black History*, pp. 7–8. On the competition for the appointment, see Labor Department, files 8–102A and 8–102B.

13. J. E. Johnson (a member of the Council of National Defense) to Joseph P. Tumulty, March 2, 1918, Labor Department, file 8–102B; W. E. B. DuBois to Louis F. Post, April 16, 1918; Emmett Scott to James H. Dillard, March 25, 1918, both in *ibid.*, file 8–102B. Scott said the appointment of Jackson would be "a calamity" and he asked Dillard: "Can you not do something to avert this travesty. There are powerful political interests pushing this man."

14. William B. Wilson to George Haynes, April 18, 1918, Labor Department, file 8–102A. A good place to gain an appreciation of the symbolic importance of these appointments is in Scott, *Scott's Official History*, chaps. 3, 4, and 26.

15. William B. Wilson to George Haynes, July 1, 1919, Labor Department, file 8–102; *Congressional Record*, 66 Cong., 2nd Sess., 6879–6880; *House Doc. No. 930*, 66th Cong., 3rd Sess. See also, *Seventh Annual Report of the Secretary of Labor, July 30, 1919* (Washington, D. C., 1919), p. 122–124; and *Eighth Annual Report of the Secretary of Labor, June 30, 1920* (Washington, D. C., 1920), pp 68–70. The ninth annual report makes no mention of the Division of Negro Economics.

16. Emmett Scott to Grosvenor B. Clarkson, March 26, 1919, Labor Department, file 8–102.

17. *Ibid*. Grosvenor B. Clarkson to Emmett Scott, March 31, 1919, Labor Department, file 8–102.

18. Meier and Rudwick, *Black History*, p. 9.

19. Carter G. Woodson, *A Century of Negro Migration* (Washington, D.C.: Association for the Study of Negro Life and History, 1918), preface, pp. 167–192.

20. *Ibid.*, preface, 167–170; Emmett J. Scott, *Negro Migration During the War* (New York: Oxford University Press, 1920), p. v; Monroe N. Work, "The Negro Migration," *The Southern Workman*, 53 (May 1924), 202–212; Charles S. Johnson, "The Negro Migration: An Economic Interpretation," *Modern Quarterly*, 2 (1925), 314–326; George Haynes, "Negroes Move North: I. Their Departure from the South," *The Survey*, 40 (May 4, 1918), 115–122.

21. Johnson, "The Negro Migration," p. 323.

22. Meier and Rudwick, *Black History*, pp. 14, 16; Emmett J. Scott (ed.), "Letters of Negro Migrants of 1916–1918," *Journal of Negro History*, 4 (July and October 1919), 290–340, 412–465.

82   *William Cohen*

23. See the citations in note 20 above.

24. Woodson, *A Century of Negro Migration*, p. 168; Scott, *Negro Migration*, p. 16.

25. *Ibid.*, pp. 6, 13. See also, Woodson, *A Century of Negro Migration*, pp. 167–171, 184–185.

26. Johnson, "The Negro Migration," p. 321. See also, Charles S. Johnson, "How Much Is The Migration a Flight From Persecution?" *Opportunity* 1 (September 1923), 272– 274.

27. *Ibid.*, p. 316.

28. John Bracey, Jr., August Meier, and Elliot Rudwick (eds.), *The Black Sociologists: The First Half Century* (Belmont, CA: Wadsworth Publishing Co., 1917), pp. 5–8; Fred H. Matthews, *Quest for an American Sociology: Robert E. Park* (Montreal: McGill-Queens University Press, 1977), p. 177.

29. Bracey, *The Black Sociologists*, pp. 7–8. Occasionally, Johnson would express his egalitarian views sharply and directly. Concluding *Patterns of Negro Segregation* (New York: Harper, 1943) he wrote that "there can be no group segregation without discrimination, and discrimination is neither democratic nor Christian." (p. 318). See also Patrick J. Gilpin, "Charles S. Johnson: An Intellectual Biography," (Ph.D. diss., Vanderbilt University, 1973), p. 113.

Neil R. McMillen

The Migration and Black Protest in Jim Crow Mississippi

The story of the Great Migration is among the most dramatic and compelling chapters in all of American history. A folk movement of incalcuable moment, it transformed not only the face of the South and the texture of African-American life, but the very character of American institutions and values. Indeed, so far-reaching are its effects that even now we scarcely understand its meaning for this state, this region, this multi-racial nation. Least of all do we appreciate the place of the black diaspora in the freedom struggle, in that protracted movement for full citizenship that began on seventeenth-century slave ships, and that continues in our time.

In this essay, I explore what might be called a forgotten chapter in the migration story—the history of those who did not migrate and their place in the black protest tradition.[1] The focus is on Mississippi during the period between the two world wars. But these observations about the search for black gain in white self-interest during the interwar period might be applied to every state in the great southern black belt. This essay will also provide a fuller historical perspective on the black struggle and on the less immediate origins of the civil rights revolution of the 1960s.

But first, a word or two about understanding the black past and, more specifically, about understanding black protest: One of this nation's problems, is that its people, black and white, know too little about their own history. Consider, for example, *Mississippi Burning*, the searing and fictionalized portrait of the 1964 Freedom Summer murders of three civil rights workers in Neshoba County. This controversial and enormously profitable box office bonanza is a timely symbol of the deficiencies of our national social memory. There is much in this film that is important and true. But by romanticizing the FBI and understating the role of blacks, the art in *Mississippi Burning* imitates not life but popular assumptions about life, assumptions born of ignorance about even the recent past.

The opening scene sets the stage for the film's subsequent errors. In real life, though not in this first scene, James Chaney, the black freedom fighter, was driving the automobile intercepted by the Klan mob that killed Chaney and his two co-workers, Schwerner and Goodman. By placing Goodman, a white northerner, in the driver's seat and Chaney in the seat behind, the director unwittingly reveals at the outset of an otherwise powerful film his own flawed assumption about the freedom struggle in Mississippi and the role of blacks in their own liberation. In this film, blacks are the objects of dramatic conflict, not the subjects; in this film, blacks are represented as victims, not as actors in their own right, not even as major players in their own story.

We should all know otherwise. We should know, not simply that FBI agents in real life were not necessarily the good guys, but that the civil rights victories of the 1960s were not delivered to black America on a federal silver platter. We should all know that the civil rights movement began at home—that its leadership and its rank and file in Mississippi were not imported into Mississippi, they were born and raised here.

And while we are listing these "should knows," we should all remember that black anger, black impatience, black militance did not just somehow materialize magically out of nowhere in 1964, or even in 1954. We should all know that civil rights protest was not somehow invented by Mrs. Parks on 1 December 1955 aboard the Cleveland Avenue bus in downtown Montgomery. We should never forget that when whites from J. Edgar Hoover to Ross Barnett and George Wallace attributed southern black unrest in the 1960s to "outside agitators," they were revealing not social reality but their own profound ignorance of black southerners and of African-American history.

And one final "should know"—perhaps the most important of all. As we study the past, we should try to avoid the sin of presentism—of measuring the past by our standards. Said another way, if we would understand black protest in an age much less favoring than our own, we must understand the practical realities of that time. We must begin with the recognition that the freedom struggles since World War II had no precise parallels in the period before World War II. Although the nadir period, the dark years of Jim Crow, are rich in the history of black resistance, black resistance in those years lacked the high drama, perhaps even the sense of heroic purpose, of the later civil rights revolution. With the notable exception of the 1904 streetcar boycotts—a statewide black users' strike that lasted in some cities for three months[2]—the half-century after 1890 experienced no direct-action campaigns. Black Mississippians in these melancholy years frequently demanded fair play and social justice. They were not foolhardy, however, and they rarely forgot the power realities of their time and place. In the 1960s, Mississippi became a laboratory in which civil rights activists displayed their most creative energies. But in the oppressive Jim Crow years, neither massive street demonstrations against economic and educational discrimination nor voter registration campaigns designed to stir the disfranchised black masses were within the realm of possibilities. Segregated, excluded, despised, and disfranchised—caught in the snares of a system designed to stifle their initiative, ensure their poverty and illiteracy, and render them politically powerless—black Mississippians in the Age of Jim Crow were poorly situated to articulate forcefully their own grievances, much less to engage in open, direct confrontation with their well-armed oppressors. Without the favorable interplay of a series of national and international developments during and after World War II, effective, sustained, direct black challenge to white supremacy was impossible in any state, least of all in Mississippi.

The point, then, is not that black Mississippians in the period between the two world wars did not resist white supremacy, but rather that they resisted with the tools then available to them—

tools stikingly different and far less availing than those of a subsequent generation. In sum, if we would understand black protest in the Jim Crow years, we must necessarily begin with an appreciation of its feasible limits. We must understand that if we look for too much we may see too little.

A consideration of black protest in the interwar years—the years that marked the onset of the Great Migration—is instructive. It is widely understood that the "great northern drive," as some called the exodus, was black protest—black protest against the outrages of lynching and injustice in the courts, protest against white notions of black character and potential, protest against the disfranchisement, the discrimination, the exclusion, and the segregation that defined the black place in what was then often called "a white man's country." Denied access to the normal democratic channels of political and social protest, migrating blacks voted with their feet, voted the only way they could, taking their talents, their energies, and their aspirations to a new promised land beyond the Ohio where, as generations of black expatriates dared to hope, the measure of human worth might be brains and character, not skin color.

That much of the migration story is now very nearly conventional wisdom. Much less is known, however, about what the exodus meant for those who stayed. Yet the conclusion seems unavoidable: the Great Migration was always more than an expression of discontent by the departing, it was also an instrument for social leverage manipulated by those blacks who did not leave. In fact, much of the meaning of the Great Migration is to be found in the response of the nonmigrants, in the little-known history of those resourceful black southerners who found advantage in white disadvantage, who developed subtle but effective tools for black protest in an age when more confrontational forms of protest would have been virtually unthinkable. Understood in this way, the onset of the Great Migration and the first world war that was its impetus can be seen as a watershed in southern history, as something of a new turning point in southern race relations, as the point of departure for what I have elsewhere described as the last leg of a dark journey through the Jim Crow years. Understood in this way, the stay-at-home generation of the Great War and the Great Migration can be seen as the precocious vanguard of the black revolution following World War II.

Obviously, to make this argument we must confront one of the standard myths regarding the social costs of the migration—that those who stayed were somehow more complacent, less aspiring, less discontent than those who went. Precisely because the exodus was the march of the impatient, precisely because it carried off many of those least satisfied with Jim Crow, too many have assumed that it drained the state of its best black stock, its most capable and intelligent black role models and community leaders. Paradoxically, although contemporary white Mississippians usually agreed that the migrants were "shiftless" and "no-account," they often also took comfort in the notion that the first to leave were the most "ambitious," "aggressive," and "uppity" blacks— those most likely to rock the racial boat. (White supremacy was never rational or logical.) Even sympathetic observers, even black Mississippians themselves, sometimes worried about the devitalizing effects of the out-migration on the remaining black community. Since flight from this latter-day bondage often required considerable self-sacrifice, since it required a driving ambition and no small courage, it has often been surmised that those who didn't make the sacrifice or take the risk didn't have the drive, didn't hate white supremacy enough to chance a new life in a strange land.

Obviously, this kind of speculation is simply that: speculation —at best unprovable, at worst defamatory of nonmigrants. But like most myths, the myth of the devitalized surviving community has some foundation in fact, for the exodus was in some respects measurably selective. Census records reveal that those with at least a high school education were more likely to go than were those less educationally advantaged. Moreover, like most migrations, this migration **did** carry off a disproportionate number of adults in their most productive years; it **did** leave behind an excess of children and old people; and it **did**, therefore, require the remaining young adult population to assume, at an increased per capita rate, the responsibilities of leadership and the costs of family and community institutions.[3]

Beyond these few facts, however, little more can be confidently said about the selective character and the social costs of the Great Migration. For if the migration left behind disproportionate numbers of the young, the old, the poorly educated, it does not follow that those who stayed were somehow more complacent or less ambitious than those who went. And if, as many whites clearly hoped, the exodus acted as something of a racial safety valve, if it siphoned off the most malcontented, aspiring, and protest-minded blacks, it did so imperfectly. The decision to leave in search of fuller participation in American life was perhaps the clearest and most frequently exercised expression of southern black discontent. But it was a relatively costly and wrenching option beyond the reach of many and one that even some of the most alienated black Mississippians did not choose to exercise. Hundreds of thousands left, including many of the most visible and articulate critics of white supremacy. But many more, not less alienated, stayed at home. If the history of the interwar period in Mississippi demonstrates anything, it is surely that these stay-at-homes, these nonmigrating black Mississippians, were neither contented nor docile.

Quite simply, the "great northern drive" created new possibilities for those who stayed as well as for those who left. With labor in short supply and whites more acutely sensitive to their dependence on black workers than at any time since emancipation, black Mississippians during World War I and the interwar period found increased opportunities to press their demands for better conditions. Although some conservative race spokesmen urged their people to stay at home, others discreetly encouraged the exodus, recognizing in the white need for black labor a chance to wring concessions from the dominant race.

In his wartime investigations in the state for the Department of Labor, a white Mississippi native discovered in 1917 that—though black leaders found it imprudent to say so publicly—they expected to manipulate white self-interest to black advantage. "At heart they rejoice over it," the white man discovered. "They are silently hoping that the migration may continue in such increasing proportions as to bring about a . . . bloodless revolution. . . . [in white behavior]."[4] Indeed, the exodus was so pregnant with possibilities that blacks from every station eagerly conspired to advance the movement out. They did so in varied ways, by sharing newspapers and other communications from the North, by protecting those who found it necessary or useful to slip away unannounced, by concealing the movements of the labor agents so hated and feared by whites, and by entering into the subterfuge of the allegedly chastened "returnees"—those dissembling returned black migrants who were, as one black Mississippian put it, "nine times out of ten" busily recruiting black workers for northern industries even as they pleased local whites by describing the horrors of Yankee life.[5]

Even blacks who opposed the migration sometimes seized the moment to emphasize the planters' obligation to treat their hands fairly. In December 1916, Dr. Joseph E. Walker, one of the state's most prominent black physicians and businessmen (a banking and insurance pioneer), used Sunflower County's leading white newspaper to encourage blacks to remain at home lest they find themselves in "a strange land among strangers . . . [with] the demons of hunger and cold, constantly prowling about their door." But Dr. Walker also delicately reminded whites of the link between the exodus and the "many conditions in the South . . . that ought to be remedied"—not least among these, the white habit of cheating black sharecroppers.[6]

Toward the same end, Valley Lester, a conservative religious and fraternal leader from Montgomery County, assumed the role of the cunning, manipulating Sambo—or perhaps of the trickster, con artist Brer Rabbit fooling the powerful but easily gulled Big White Wolf. Whatever Lester's guise, the artful black man instructed whites in 1919 on their Christian duties in terms that could hardly be misunderstood:

> My race works your streets, my race enjoys being your servants, they loved to bring in the bales of cotton for you in the fall of the year. [But a man of] my race [also] . . . wants you to prove that you are his friend by the kindly and friendly way which you have treated him.

In his wileist "white folks' manner," Lester heaped praise on white benevolence, extolled the "great southland" as "the finest of all" regions, and urged the black field hand to "stay where you are, . . . work on halves or for wages. . . ." But his circumlocutions also included a scarcely veiled warning that whites must mend their ways or pick their own cotton: "The southern negro only wants . . . fair and honest treatment and we are willing to forever stay at home and let the north be the north. . . ."[7]

Black candor, of course, was usually tightly constrained by the realistic fear of white retaliation. But if black Mississippians could not always be forthright, they could be resourceful and they could and did find ways to identify out-migration with black unrest, with the black wish for full citizenship and equal justice.

Above all, black Mississippians understood that pressure from their community could be counterproductive. Those who used the migration crisis to bargain for improved conditions generally found it more fruitful to appeal to white pocketbooks than to white consciences. Thus, when the Warren County Colored Ministers' Association petitioned local authorities in 1918 for better black rural schools, black clergy emphasized the relationship between agricultural prosperity and a contented workforce. Existing black education facilities "are not such as might breed contentment," the ministers stated. "We have noticed that the people . . . are not settled. Many are leaving."[8]

Perhaps the most dramatic endeavors to convert crisis into opportunity came from a series of conventions that met in the state during the war and early postwar period. In 1918, for example, a delegation of some fifty blacks appeared before the education committee of the state House of Representatives to request that black elementary, secondary, and college students be given the same eduation opportunities as whites. "If these matters are given substantial consideration . . ." group spokesman Perry Howard (then a Jackson attorney) assured the lawmakers, "the exodus which has struck at the very foundation of the labor system of Mississippi will be largely checked. . . ."[9]

The statements of the black conventions organized by Jackson attorney and physician Sidney D. Redmond in 1923 and 1924 were more direct. Identifying "a few of the many reasons which cause the Negro to . . . leave the State," these leadership conferences drafted catalogs of black grievances that ranged from mob violence and injustice in the courts to exploitative labor practices and educational inequalities, to neglected public services and disfranchisement. Affirming their own deep interest "in the future welfare of the commonwealth," the conferees concluded in 1923 that "there is no hope whatever of bringing back the Negroes who have already left the State . . . the only hope now lies in taking the proper steps to retain as many as possible of those who are [still] here."[10]

Although much of this postwar protest was improvisational, ad hoc and ephemeral in nature, some of it was well organized, highly structured, and continuing. The most representative institutional expressions of the new opportunism were the underappreciated Mississippi Federation of Colored Women's Clubs and the now-all-but-forgotten Committe of One Hundred. Both were race uplift organizations that fused black self-help and prudent social agitation, and both found new ways to manipulate white self-interest to black advantage. Neither has received due recognition as the protest organization that it was.

The Women's Federation, of course, could trace its origins to 1903, when the wives of Mississippi's black business, professional, educational, and religious leaders met in Jackson to form a movement that survives to this very day. At the local level, club women generally focused on the traditional concerns of middle-class women's organizations: health, home, school, and church. At the state level, however, the work of the Federation was more race-conscious, centering on what an official history called the "cause of right and justice," particularly black demands for an equitable distribution of social services. Though its local affiliates, the Federation operated retirement homes for elderly and destitue blacks at Vicksburg and Natchez; under the leadership of such women as Grace Morris Allen Jones, Mary Booze, and Bertha LaBranche Johnson, the state organization lobbied education officials for the inclusion of libraries in black schools and for the inclusion of African-American history in black grammar school curricula; it also waged long-term campaigns to win state support for the care of black tuberculosis patients, the education of handicapped black children, and the construction of a training school for "delinquent" black youths (the latter, of course, being the Oakley Training School, which opened in 1943 after more than two decades of steady pressure from the Federation and its allies). Activities such as these may resonate less in history than do the Montgomery bus boycott or the Mississippi Summer project. But such quiet pressure as the Federation applied to the white establishment in the 1920s and 1930s helped prepare the way for the more spectacular breakthroughs of later decades.[11]

Much the same should be said of the work of the Committe of One Hundred. Formed amid a postwar surge of out-migration in 1923, the Committee took its name from its ambition to be a statewide conference of 100 leading black men and women from every county in Mississippi. Preferring to work quietly, out of public view, the organization met with white business, civic, and religious groups to "negotiate progress," express black dissatisfaction, and subtly remind the dominant race that flight from Mississippi and injustice within Mississippi were two sides of the same Jim Crow coin.

A useful example of the Committee's success in "negotiating progress" with reluctant whites comes from the early postwar period. In this case, the all-white board of trustees of Alcorn A&M College agreed to restore Latin to the school's curriculum after learning from Committee leaders that black students who would study foreign language had to do so outside of Mississippi, sometimes at integrated northern universities where they encountered "pernicious doctrines," "ideas that don't fit." Skillfully exploiting white fears, black leaders in this instance succeeded, as Committee president Jonas Edward Johnson later put it, in "turning race prejudice back on itself." Describing the triumph to his sons—all of whom attended college in other states—the shrewd black educator explained that in dealings with whites, "there is a very thin line between diplomacy and duplicity."[12]

But whether through duplicity or diplomacy, the organization had an impact. As a friendly white lawmaker informed other members of the State House of Representatives in 1923, the Committee of One Hundred sought only such improvements as would "prevent the great exodus of their people to the Northern states and get them to remain here . . . where . . . they are so much needed. . . ." Prompted by Committee spokesmen, this legislator supported increased funding for black vocational education to "show the Negroes of the State that we . . . want them to stay here in Mississippi."[13]

Other whites responded to similar pressures—testifying, often unwittingly, to the effectiveness of the nonmigrants' strategy. Calling for moderate social redress, scattered and sometimes prominent white voices addressed the issues of most pressing black concern: the inadequacy of black schools, the poverty and indebtedness of virtually all tenants, the record of unpunished white lawlessness, and a general white disposition to (as some put it) "keep the nigger down." In 1920, for example, the Mississippi Department of the American Legion urged members of its local posts to "put forth their best effort for the promotion of harmony between the races"; in 1923, perhaps the peak interwar year of black out-migration, the state Chamber of Commerce called upon white business and civic leaders in every community to make such adjustments as might slow the out-migration; and in 1924, in his inaugural address, Governor Henry L. Whitfield directly linked the welfare of the state's black majority to the welfare of the state as a whole. "Our own self interest," the governor declared, requires a "new era" of race relations on the plantations, in the schools, and in the courts.[14]

These remarkable examples of self-reproof were not widely emulated. Although some optimistic observers detected a "more enlightened" strain of white thought, even a "new age of altruism,"[15] the spirit of white accommodation, meager as it was, scarcely survived the critical labor shortages of the war and its early aftermath. By 1918, labor market adjustments pushed up black agricultural and industrial wages across the state 10 to 30 percent. Sawmill hands, steamboat workers, and Piney Woods lumberjacks were promised "good labor conditions," improved management and safety practices, and better housing. During the war and into the early 1920s, planters offered tenants improved living quarters, somewhat greater autonomy, and more varied and healthful diets. Representatives of both races agreed that sharecropper settlements were, for the moment, often fairer and that the lash was applied more sparingly on many plantations. Police in a number of communities were instructed to deal less harshly with black offenders, and in some areas blacks were said to receive more even-handed justice in the courts. Nearly everywhere in the state, whites seemed momentarily more attentive to black educational demands. Most promising of all, whites in a number of rural communities talked openly of the need for better treatment of black agricultural workers and sometimes white civic and business leaders even met with leading blacks to discuss questions of "mutual welfare."[16]

In most cases, these conferences produced little more than paternalistic rhetoric and probably wounded more black feelings than they healed. All too typically, a "better race relations" meeting sponsored by the earnest white ladies of Vicksburg began with "a brief address on our duties as superiors toward our inferiors of the colored race" and progressed to adjurations for more sympathetic treatment of black workers "so that they will be perfectly content to stay in the south, the section best suited to their advancement."[17]

Other endeavors, however, including the widely celebrated but short-lived Bolivar County "Community Congress," resulted if only briefly in what some thought to be "better [race] feelings." Composed of twenty whites and five blacks, this planter-dominated Congress met only a few times during the war and was hardly democratic in design. Yet it provided a formal vehicle for interracial contact and can probably be credited with the postwar construction of the state's first black agricultural high school.[18]

To be sure, the fruits of these interracial conclaves were rarely so tangible. Blacks generally viewed such concessions as the grudging expedients that they were and accepted the white man's new found attentions with a mixture of appreciation and amusement. As one black Mississippian told a visiting scholar following a meeting with local whites: "The dominant race is just a bit less dominant at present."[19] Yet if they found their working conditions momentarily more tolerable, black Mississippians were too seasoned in the ways of white supremacy to expect immediate major adjustments in a system designed to keep them subordinate. Nor were they surprised in the postwar period when white interest in conciliation waned about as quickly as labor shortages eased.

What then can be made of all this? It need hardly be said that the exploitation of white self-interest by non-migrating blacks —however resourceful—did not in the years between the two world wars revolutionize race relations in Mississippi. Despite some modest black gains, the essential contours of white supremacy remained intact well into the 1960s—and even now, nearly twenty-five years after the implementation of the Voting Rights Act, the civil rights revolution remains America's unfinished revolution.

Yet if these nonmigrants, these quiet reformers of the interwar years, did not precisely win—if they did not manage to topple Jim Crow in their generation—history also shows that they did not struggle in vain and that they did not fail. The black effort to capitalize on the Great Migration was one piece of a larger pattern of black protest. As close examination of the interwar years reveals, these stay-at-home Mississippians participated in a growing struggle against Jim Crow. Although the full story of that struggle cannot be told here, the developments described in this essay need to be placed in a larger context.

To do so, we must return to the idea of World War I as a racial watershed. That war signaled the beginning of a journey toward freedom, the early departure point for the freedom struggles of our own time. The spirit of social change fostered by the first world war touched the Mississippi homefront in ways that could not be reversed. The call to service in the armed forces, in the defense industry, and in civilian patriotic work, quickened black pride, expanded black horizons, and otherwise disrupted the patterns of a static society. To be sure, the black expectation that patriotic sacrifice would result in significant changes was premature. Yet the war and the early period of the migration nevertheless marked the beginnings of a gathering challenge to the old order. In the interwar years black Mississippians escalated their demands for broader citizenship rights. Many left the state, and many others used that exodus in creative ways. A surprising number quietly joined local chapters of the Universal Negro Improvement Association, suggesting that Garveyism was much more than the northern inner-city phenomenon historians once thought it to be. Beginning in 1918, others turned to a few scattered and generally short-lived underground branches of the NAACP and the feeble state council of the Committee on Interracial Cooperation. Others pursued the nonagitational strategies of the Federation of Colored Women's Clubs and the Committee of One Hundred.

To a more expectant generation coming of age following World War II, the activism of these interwar reformers seemed too accommodative, almost pallid. A more reasoned judgment, however, suggests that they were about as assertive as their time and place permitted, and that they succeeded in developing new channels of interracial communication, in contributing importantly to the evolution of a bolder black agenda, and in pressing black demands for social justice as no black Mississippians had since the aftermath of Reconstruction. More aggressive tactics and more militant demands would have been perhaps suicidal and most certainly counterproductive. As one elderly black educator explained recently, "Had Mississippi blacks pushed in the 1920s like they did in the 1960s, they would have been slaughtered."[20]

That, of course, is precisely the point—and the all-important qualifier to the argument here. There were no dramatic breakthroughs in this interwar period. Black malcontent and protest, though rising steadily, characteristically flowed underground, undetected even by watchful whites, or in relatively safe and nonconfrontational channels. Voteless black Mississippians did not march in the streets for suffrage and their demands for justice normally called for equality within separation, not racial integration. Social movements, after all, have social contexts, and the character of social agitation, like the pace of social change itself, is conditioned by the environment in which it functions. Whatever else one might conclude from a study of the Jim Crow years, it is surely that an effective, broad-based, sustained social justice movement of, by, and for blacks could not have developed anywhere in the South without salutary changes in the larger national and international intellectual and political milieu in which American racial attitudes, social policies, and interracial behaviors are shaped.

Necessarily, then, the first world war was a turning point that turned only slightly. It heightened race consciousness and black unrest; it contributed to a reconfiguration of the race problem nationwide; it hastened the developmental processes and the generational changes that modified black circumstances, diminished white control, and ultimately made possible a fundamental transformation of American race relations. Almost unnoticed, the forces of reform mounted, making the gathering black challenge an impending revolution, making the interwar generation of black activism in Mississippi the bridge between pre–World War I Booker Washington–style accommodationism and post–World War II civil rights protest, making the period of the Great War and the onset of the Great Migration the prelude to a much larger, more powerful drama of human struggle that could unfold only as national and international developments permitted.

That drama, of course, would little resemble *Mississippi Burning*. In life, if too rarely in the movies, blacks would be the primary players. In real life, black Mississippians in the aftermath of World War II redefined the limits of protest and reimagined their place in a democratic nation. Recognizing that time and circumstance were at last on their side, convinced of the possibility and the necessity for new strategies of opposition to white supremacy, they entered the postwar period prepared in heart and mind for the assault on Jim Crow. As one of them informed a northern journalist, their own emergent tradition of unrest and social agitation propelled them ineluctably toward the increasingly militant protest movement of the 1950s and 1960s: "Lord child," this stay-at-home woman told a northern writer, "we colored people [in Mississippi] ain't nothing but a bundle of resentments and suffering going somewhere to explode."[21]

1. That story is more fully told in Neil R. McMillen, *Dark Journey: Black Mississippians in the Age of Jim Crow* (Urbana: University of Illinois Press, 1989).

2. August Meier and Elliott Rudwick, "The Boycott Movement against Jim Crow Streetcars in the South, 1900–1906," in Meier and Rudwick, *Along the Color Line: Explorations in the Black Experience* (Urbana: University of Illinois Press, 1976), 267–289.

3. See Daniel O. Price, "Education Differentials between Negroes and Whites in the South," *Demography*, 5 (1968), 32; C. Horace Hamilton, "The Negro Leaves the South," *Demography*, 1 (1964), 284–285, 289; idem, "Educational Selectivity of Net Migration from the South," *Social Forces*, 38 (October, 1959), 35; Elizabeth M. Suval and C. Horace Hamilton, "Some New Evidence of Educational Selectivity in Migration from the South," *Social Forces*, 43 (May, 1965), 536–547; Hope T. Eldridge and Dorothy S. White, *Demographic Analyses and Interrelations*, 204, vol. 3 of Simon Kuznets *et al.*, *Population Redistribution and Economic Growth: United States, 1870–1950* (Philadelphia: American Philosophical Society, 1957).

4. U.S. Department of Labor, *Negro Migration in 1916–1917: Reports* (Washington, D.C.: Government Printing Office, 1919), 32 (quotation); *American Missionary*, new ser., 9 (July, 1919), 223; Jackson *Daily News*, January 7, 1920.

5. U.S. Department of Labor, *Negro Migration in 1916–1917*, 28; Emmett J. Scott, *Negro Migration During the War* (New York: Oxford University Press, 1920), 37.

6. Sunflower *Tocsin*, December 7, 1916. For similar arguments, see also Isaiah T. Montgomery, *Our Great State, Mississippi: Tragic Sketch of the Past, the Great Turmoil of the Present, and the Wonderful Possibilities of the Future* (Mound Bayou: J. W. Covington, [1923]), passim.

7. Valley L. Lester, *The Mob Violence and the American Negro* (Winona, Miss.: Dublin Printing Company, 1919), 38, 52–53.

8. Vicksburg *Evening Post*, December 2, 1918. Similar statements appear in Meridian *Star*, April 5, 1917; and Memphis *Commercial-Appeal*, September 9, 1917.

9. Jackson *Daily Clarion-Ledger*, February 23, 28, 1918.

10. Press release, Citizens' Mass Convention, May 2, 1923, box C-373, NAACP Papers, Library of Congress, Washington, D.C.; "Negroes Say Why They Leave the South," *American Missionary*, new ser., 15 (September, 1923), 293; Jackson *Daily News*, January 29, 1924. See also Redmond's document prepared for the legislature in 1926: *Crisis*, 32 (December, 1926), 102.

11. Grace Morris Allen Jones, *What the Mississippi Women Are Doing* (Braxton, Miss.: Piney Woods School Printing Department, [1922?]), 3–12; "History of the Mississippi Association of Colored Women," *National Association of Colored Women, Inc., 1891–1952* (n.p., n.d.), 86–94; Mrs. M. M. Hubert, "Club Women's View on National Health Week," *National Negro Health News*, 3 (April–June, 1935), 3–5; J. E. Johnson to Dear Friend, January 20, 1934, and Minutes, Annual Meeting of the Committee of One Hundred, December 16, 1933, Jonas E. Johnson Papers, in possession of Alcee L. Johnson, Prentiss, Mississippi (hereinafter cited as JEJ).

12. Interviews with Alcee L. Johnson, October 16, November 15, 1986 (quotation). The Committee's history has been recounted in some detail in McMillen, *Dark Journey*, 278, 280, 302, 309–311; but see also J. B. F., "The Story of the Committee," [1934], unpaginated, and the reports and minutes of the organization in JEJ; Montgomery, *Our Great State*, app., 6–7; Prentiss, *Spirit of Mississippi*, June 1, 1934.

13. O. C. Luper to Dear Representative, December 31, 1923, JEJ.

14. Jackson *Daily News*, October 27, 1923; Arvarh E. Strickland, "To the Manor Born: Southern White Responses to Black Migration in the 1920s" (Paper delivered at the Fifty-second Annual meeting of the Southern Historical Association, Charolttesville, Va., November 1986), 13; Mississippi Senate *Journal*, 1924, 200–201; Lester A. Walton, "Whitfield—Apostle of Racial Good Will," *Outlook*, 136 (April 9, 1924), 589–591.

15. P. P. Garner to Jessie O. Thomas, January 20, 1926, and R. S. Curry to Thomas, January 16, 1926, Central Office file, box A-19, National Urban League Papers, Library of Congress.

16. Scott, *Negro Migration*, 83–84, 87, 89; Jonathan Daniels, *A Southerner Discovers the South* (New York: Macmillan Company, 1938), 178–179; Howard Snyder, "Plantation Pictures," *Atlantic Monthly*, 127 (February, 1921), 169–170.

17. Quoted in Vicksburg *Evening Post*, September 14, 1918.

18. New York *Age*, March 15, 1919; U.S. Department of Labor, *Negro Migration in 1916–1917*, 46; Scott, *Negro Migration*, 83–84; Pete Daniel, *Breaking the Land: The Transformation of Cotton, Tobacco, and Rice Cultures since 1880* (Urbana: University of Illinois Press, 1985), 12; Edwin Mims, comp., *A Handbook of Inter-Racial Committees* (n.p., 1926), 7.

19. Quoted in Scott, *Negro Migration*, 90.

20. Interview with Alcee L. Johnson, November 15, 1986.

21. Quoted in Louis E. Lomax, *The Negro Revolt*, rev. ed. (New York: Harper and Row, Perennial Library, 1971), 92.

Contributors

Blyden Jackson is professor of literature emeritus at the University of North Carolina at Chapel Hill. His publications include *The Waiting Years* (1976) and with Louis Rubin, *Black Poetry in America* (1974) and editor, with Louis Rubin *et al.*, of *The History of Southern Literature* (1985).

Dernoral Davis is assistant professor of history at Jackson State University. His publications include "To Go or Stay: The Issue of Black Migration in the Twentieth Century," *Those Who Stayed: A Collectanea* (1989).

Stewart E. Tolnay is associate professor of sociology at the State University of New York at Albany and E. M. Beck is associate professor of sociology at the University of Georgia. Their publications include "The Killing Fields of the Deep South: The Market For Cotton and the Lynching of Blacks, 1882–1930," *American Sociological Review*, 1990; and "The Gallows, The Mob, The Vote: Lethal Sanctioning of Blacks in North Carolina and Georgia, 1882–1930," *Law and Society Review*, 1989 (with J. L. Massey).

Carole Marks is assistant professor of Black American Studies and Sociology at the University of Delaware in Newark. She is author of *Farewell We're Good and Gone: The Great Black Migration*.

James R. Grossman, director of the Newberry Library's Family and Community History Center, is author of *Land of Hope: Black Southerners, Chicago and the Great Migration* and editor of *Black Workers in the Era of the Great Migration, 1916–1929*.

William Cohen, professor of history at Hope College in Holland, Michigan, has completed a manuscript entitled *At Freedom's Edge: Black Mobility and the Southern White Quest for Racial Control, 1862–1915.*

Neil McMillen is professor of history at the University of Southern Mississippi. His *Dark Journey: Black Mississippians in the Age of Jim Crow, 1890–1940* was awarded the 1990 Bancroft Prize in American history.

Index